Study Guide to Accompany

The Professional Chef
Ninth Edition

The Culinary Institute of America

WILEY

JOHN WILEY & SONS, INC.

This book is printed on acid-free paper.

Copyright © 2011 by The Culinary Institute of America. All rights reserved

Published by John Wiley & Sons, Inc., Hoboken, New Jersey
Published simultaneously in Canada

For general information on our other products and services or for technical support, please contact our Customer Care Department within the United States at (800) 762-2974, outside the United States at (317) 572-3993 or fax (317) 572-4002.

Wiley also publishes its books in a variety of electronic formats. Some content that appears in print may not be available in electronic books. For more information about Wiley products, visit our web site at www.wiley.com.

This material may be reproduced for testing or instructional purposes by instructors using the text The Professional Chef, Ninth Edition by The Culinary Institute of America, 9780470421352.

Library of Congress Cataloging-in-Publication Data:

ISBN-10: 1118139887
ISBN-13: 9781118139882

Printed in the United States of America

SKY10037303_102522

Contents

CHAPTER **1**

Chapter Overview

Culinary professionals today have more opportunities than ever before, both in and out of the kitchen. Although a basic culinary education is of fundamental importance, a successful culinarian will work to develop new skills, attributes, and talents throughout his or her career.

Chapter Objectives

After reading and studying this chapter, you will be able to:

➤ Cite and describe the attributes of a culinary professional

➤ Knowledgably discuss the chef's role as a businessperson

➤ Describe four areas in which chefs must be managers

➤ List various types of foodservice establishments

➤ Explain the background and importance of a kitchen and dining room brigade system

➤ Name and describe a variety of culinary career opportunities

Study Outline

Becoming a Culinary Professional

Key Terms and Concepts

accredited school	apprenticeship	career development
networking	self-directed study	training

The Attributes of a Culinary Professional

Key Terms and Concepts

commitment to service	sense of responsibility	sound judgment

The Chef as Businessperson

Key Terms and Concepts

Administrator	communication	executive
human resources information	manager	physical assets
time	training	work environment

Career Opportunities for Culinary Professionals

Key Terms and Concepts

caterer
home meal replacement
private club

executive dining room
hotel

full-service restaurant
institutional catering

The Kitchen Brigade System

Key Terms and Concepts

brigade
cold-foods chef
executive chef
fry chef
roast chef
sous chef

butcher
commis
expediter
grill chef
roundsman
vegetable chef

chef de cuisine
communard
fish chef
pastry chef
sauté chef

The Dining Room Brigade System

Key Terms and Concepts

back waiter
front waiter
wine steward

captain
head waiter

dining room manager
maître d'hôtel

Other Opportunities

Key Terms and Concepts

consultant
food and beverage manager
photographer
teacher

critic
food stylist
research and development

design specialist
food writer
salesperson

Chapter 1 Exercises

True/False

Indicate whether each of the following statements is True (T) or False (F)

_____ 1. The management of human resources is rarely the responsibility of the chef.

_____ 2. Physical assets in a restaurant or food service operation include all equipment and supplies needed to do business.

_____ 3. An important strategy for managing time is to learn to communicate clearly.

_____ 4.   Hotel facilities often have separate butchering, catering, and pastry kitchens on premises to service all their operations.

_____ 5.   Under the brigade system, in a large pastry operation, the role of pastry chef might be broken down into several stations including confiseur, boulanger, glacier, and décorateur.

_____ 6.   In the brigade system, the vegetable chef, or entremetier, might be responsible for vegetables, hot appetizers, soups, pastas, starches, and egg dishes.

_____ 7.   Following the positions of executive chef and sous chef, the role of sauté chef is considered the most demanding, responsible, and glamorous position on the line.

_____ 8.   In the brigade system, all appetizers are prepared by the vegetable chef (entremetier).

_____ 9.   Under the classic brigade system, in the absence of a fish chef, the responsibilities of that station typically fall to the grill or roast station.

_____ 10. Medical and dental insurance are optional benefits that might be offered to employees; they are not legal requirements.

Multiple Choice

Circle the single best answer for each

11. The garde-manger is responsible for
    a.   cold food preparation.
    b.   hot appetizers, and possibly soups.
    c.   all grilled foods.
    d.   preparing the staff or "family" meal.

12. The front-of-the-house staff member who works most closely with the chef is the
    a   front waiter.
    b.   captain.
    c.   maître d'hôtel.
    d.   sommelier.

13. The key components for creating a positive work environment are
    a.   employees benefits packages.
    b.   job description and training.
    c.   inventory control systems.
    d.   adult literacy programs and continuing education.

14. The type of insurance which must be purchased to cover any harm to your facility, employees, or guests is known as
    a. workers' compensation.
    b. medical insurance.
    c. liability insurance.
    d. disability insurance.

15. In a hotel or large establishment, the person who oversees all food and beverage outlets is the
    a. sous chef.
    b. food and beverage manager.
    c. controller.
    d. maître d'hôtel.

Fill in the Blank
For each space, insert the most appropriate response

16. In the brigade system, the _____ is responsible for fish items, often including fish butchering, and their sauces. This position is sometimes combined with the _____ position.

17. In the brigade system, the _____ is responsible for all roasted foods, and related jus and sauces. In a small operation, this chef may also take on the responsibilities of the _____ and _____.

18. As a culinary professional progresses in his or her career, he or she must often become a good _____ _____, _____, and _____.

19. In order for a chef to become a good manager, he or she will need to learn to manage _____ ___, _____, _____, and _____.

20. Three primary attributes or character traits the culinary professional should strive for include _ ____, _____, and _____.

Matching
Select the single best match for each item

_____ 21. Friturier   a. Pastry chef
_____ 22. Pâtissier   b. Expediter
_____ 23. Chef de rang   c. Fry chef
_____ 24. Aboyeur   d. Captain
_____ 25. Chef d'étage   e. Front waiter
_____ 26. Glacier   f. Prepares frozen and cold desserts

Essay/Short Answer

Answer each question as fully as possible

27. Why is time management such an important skill for a chef to acquire? What are some key strategies a chef/manager can use to manage time?

_____
_____
_____
_____
_____
_____

28. How does a chef effectively manage human resources? How can he or she acquire and retain high-caliber employees?

_____
_____
_____
_____
_____
_____

29. How should one go about becoming a culinary professional? What are some important resources available?

_____
_____
_____
_____
_____
_____

30. What are some less traditional career opportunities in food service? List five and describe each job.

_____
_____
_____
_____
_____
_____

31. What are the primary attributes of a culinary professional? Discuss each.

_____

_____

_____

_____

_____

_____

CHAPTER 2

Chapter Overview

A well-designed menu is the most important tool a restaurant has. Menus are used in the dining room to give both wait staff and guests important information about what the establishment offers. Recipes give detailed instructions to aid kitchen staff in producing menu items. But, more than that, carefully designed menus and comprehensive recipes can help the professional chef streamline kitchen operations and control costs.

Chapter Objectives

After reading and studying this chapter, you will be able to:

➢ Explain what is meant by a standardized recipe

➢ Name the elements in a standard recipe and describe how they are used as effective business and management tools in the operation of a professional kitchen

➢ Measure dry and liquid ingredients properly

➢ Increase and decrease (also known as "scale") recipes to suit production needs using appropriate formulas and calculations

➢ Use basic recipe and yield calculations to determine food and recipe costs

➢ Convert from one measurement system to another

Study Outline

Menus

Key Terms and Concepts

à la carte	banquet	menu

Recipes

Key Terms and Concepts

convert	mise en place	recipe

Measuring Ingredients Accurately

Key Terms and Concepts

bunch	count	each

| measurement | volume | weight |

Standardized Recipes

Key Terms and Concepts

| portion size | published recipe | recipe elements |
| standard | standardized recipe | yield information |

Recipe Calculations

Key Terms and Concepts

as-purchased cost	as-purchased quantity	decimal system
desired yield	edible portion cost	edible portion quantity
metric system	original yield	purchase pack
recipe conversion factor	unit	U.S. system
usable trim	yield percent	

Using Recipes Effectively

Key Terms and Concepts

| efficiency | organization | profits |

The Butcher's Yield Test

Key Terms and Concepts

| cost factor | cost per portion | fabricated cost |
| fabricated price | fabricated weight | trim |

Chapter 2 Exercises

True/False

Indicate whether each of the following statements is True (T) or False (F)

_____ 1. All food items have some sort of loss, so a yield percentage must be determined for each item in the kitchen.

_____ 2. Most food items purchased from suppliers and purveyors are packed and priced by wholesale bulk prices.

_____ 3. Detailed standardized recipes serve little purpose in a small operation where one person performs most of the cooking.

_____ 4. Volume is a measure of the mass or heaviness of a solid, liquid, or gas.

_____ 5. Weight measures should be used when scaling recipes. Volume measures are suitable for all other recipe preparations.

_____ 6. Standardized recipes may be tailored to suit the needs of an individual kitchen.

_____ 7. In some cases, volume measures may be preferable to weight measures, because volume measuring tools are required to meet specific standards for accuracy.

_____ 8. The butcher's yield test allows the chef or butcher to take into account the fact that much of the trim can be used in other preparations.

_____ 9. The most accurate way to measure onions for a recipe is by count.

_____ 10. Volume measuring tools are acceptable when measuring small amounts of spices.

Multiple Choice

Circle the single best answer for each

11. The yield percentage is used to determine
    a. overall yield of any given recipe.
    b. yield per portion of any given recipe.
    c. the percentage of unusable trim in product as it is purchased.
    d. the percentage of usable product in product as it is purchased.

12. To determine the edible portion quantity (EPQ) of an item
    a. weigh all raw product and divide by the number of portions.
    b. subtract trim loss from the as-purchased cost.
    c. subtract trim loss from the as-purchased quantity.
    d. divide the as-purchased cost total by the number of units.

13. In order to determine the edible portion quantity of 2 pounds of carrots, you must
    a. trim and portion the carrots and weigh each portion.
    b. portion the carrots and divide the total cost of the carrots by the number of portions.
    c. divide the total cost of the carrots by the cost of any trim loss.
    d. trim the carrots and subtract any trim loss from the original weight.

14. Many recipes call for ingredients that are prepped and ready to cook. In order to purchase the correct amount of an item taking into account the trim loss during fabrication, you need to
    a. divide the edible portion quantity (EPQ) by the as-purchased quantity (APQ).
    b. divide the edible portion quantity (EPQ) by the yield percentage.
    c. multiply the as-purchased quantity (APQ) and the yield percentage.
    d. multiply the as-purchased quantity (APQ) and the edible portion quantity (EPQ).

15. Many recipes call for ingredients that are prepped and ready to cook. In order to determine the cost of an item taking into account the trim loss during fabrication, you need to
    a. divide the edible portion quantity (EPQ) by the edible portion cost (EPQ).
    b. divide the as-purchased cost (APC) by the yield percentage.
    c. multiply the as-purchased quantity (APQ) and the edible portion cost (EPC).
    d. multiply the edible portion cost (EPC) and the yield percentage.

Fill in the Blank

For each space, insert the most appropriate response

16. Four of the important items on a standardized recipe include _____, _____ _____, _____, and _____ (also, temperature, cooking time, and safe good handling procedures, or CCP.)

17. Before starting to cook from any recipe, the first step is to _____.

18. Ingredients are purchased and used according to one of three measuring conventions: _____ ____, _____, and _____.

19. The _____, used throughout most of the world, is a _____ meaning that it is based on multiples of 10. In America, the most common form of measure is the ____ _____.

20. When increasing or decreasing recipe yields, three things you must always consider are _____ _____, _____, and _____

Matching

Select the single best match for each item

_____ 21. Trim loss   a. EPQ divided by APQ

_____ 22. As-purchased quantity   b. As-purchased cost minus total trim value

_____ 23. Yield percentage   c. Wholesale bulk price divided by number of units

_____ 24. Cost per unit   d. The unusable portion of an item

_____ 25. Recipe conversion factor   e. The item's weight or volume at the time of purchase

_____ 26. New fabricated weight   f. Desired yield divided by original yield

Essay/Short Answer

Answer each question as fully as possible

27. What is the purpose of a menu?

_____

_____

_____

28. What is the purpose of a standardized recipe? What elements are included?

_____

_____

_____

_____

_____

_____

29. Describe the three measuring conventions used to purchase and use ingredients, noting where each convention is most appropriate.

_____

_____

_____

_____

_____

_____

30. Explain the processes for converting ounces to grams, grams to ounces, fluid ounces to milliliters, and milliliters to fluid ounces.

_____

_____

_____

_____

_____

_____

31. What is the butcher's yield test? What does it calculate?

_____

_____

_____

_____

_____

_____

CHAPTER 3

Chapter Overview

Americans are increasingly aware of the importance of proper nutrition; accordingly, the foodservice industry must respond to changing consumer needs by providing healthy options for diners. Understanding the scientific principles involved in preparing and cooking food, as well as their effects on nutrition, is an essential component of the culinary professional's job.

Chapter Objectives

After reading and studying this chapter, you will be able to:

➢ Discuss the importance of nutrition and food science to the professional chef

➢ Define nutrition and explain the role of the following: Calories, carbohydrates, fat, cholesterol, protein, vitamins, and minerals

➢ Describe the effect on foods as they cook for each of following methods of heat transfer: conduction, convection, and radiation

➢ Discuss the effects of heat on starches and sugars (caramelization, Maillard reaction, and gelatinization)

➢ Explain how denaturing proteins affects foods as they cook

➢ Define the function of cooking fats

➢ Define an emulsion and understand the two different phases within an emulsion

Study Outline

Nutrition Basics

Key Terms and Concepts

alcohol	amino acid	carbohydrate
cholesterol	complete protein	complex carbohydrate
daily caloric intake	energy	essential amino acid
fat	fat-soluble	incomplete protein
mineral	nutrient	nutrient-dense
nutrition	principles of healthy cooking	protein
vitamin	water-soluble	

Menu Development and Nutrition

Key Terms and Concepts

portion size   well-balanced meal choices

Heat Transfer

Key Terms and Concepts

conduction   convection   cooking
heat transfer   induction cooking   infrared radiation
mechanical convection   microwave radiation   natural convection
radiation

Effects of Heat on Starches and Sugars: Caramelization, Maillard Reaction, and Gelatinization

Key Terms and Concepts

caramelization   gelatinization   Maillard reaction
starch   sugar

Denaturing Proteins

Key Terms and Concepts

coagulation   denaturation   egg
lecithin   natural protein   "resting"

Function of Cooking Fats

Key Terms and Concepts

liquid fat   oil   solid fat
smoke point

Forming Emulsions

Key Terms and Concepts

continuous phase   dispersed phase   emulsifier
emulsion   stable emulsion   temporary emulsion

Chapter 3 Exercises

True/False

Indicate whether each of the following statements is True (T) or False (F)

_____ 1. Calcium is the mineral found most abundantly in the body.

_____ 2. The U.S. Department of Agriculture suggests that fat should not exceed 10 percent of total daily calories.

_____ 3. The water-soluble vitamins A, D, E, and K dissolve in water and are easily transported throughout the body in the bloodstream.

_____ 4. Dietary cholesterol is found in both animal and plant foods.

_____ 5. Vitamin C aids in the growth and maintenance of body tissue.

_____ 6. Carbohydrates are necessary for the body to work efficiently and to fulfill its energy needs.

_____ 7. In the case of obesity, it is not fat itself which is the cause of the problem, but the amount of calories consumed.

_____ 8. The Maillard reaction takes place at a much lower temperature than does caramelization.

_____ 9. During the baking process, fat aids in moisture retention.

_____ 10. The smoke points of animal fats are typically higher than those of vegetable oils.

Multiple Choice

Circle the single best answer for each

11. Fat is an essential component of a healthy diet in part because
    a. it makes certain vitamins available to the body.
    b. it provides a sensation of fullness or satiety.
    c. it is crucial in the development of flavor in cooking.
    d. it provides energy for muscle movement and red blood cells.

12. Carbohydrates are an essential component of a healthy diet in part because
    a. they make certain vitamins available to the body.
    b. they help in the growth and development of bones and teeth.
    c. they clear cholesterol out of the circulatory system.
    d. they are necessary for the body to work efficiently and to fulfill its energy needs.

13. The component which is essential for the growth and maintenance of body tissues, and the production of hormones, enzymes, and antibodies is
   a. protein.
   b. fat.
   c. carbohydrates.
   d. vitamins and minerals.

14. Serum cholesterol is
   a. healthier than dietary cholesterol.
   b. a monounsaturated fat.
   c. essential to life.
   d. stored in the liver.

15. Vegetarians who do not consume animal foods should
   a. take vitamins and minerals in supplement form.
   b. combine incomplete proteins so they can consume all essential amino acids.
   c. be careful to consume enough cholesterol in their daily meals.
   d. consume 16 to 20 percent of their calories from protein.

Fill in the Blank
For each space, insert the most appropriate response

16. The basic building blocks of protein are known as_____, of which nine are _____. A _____ contains all nine.

17. Two minerals essential to the growth and maintenance of teeth are _____ and _____.

18. Four culinary functions of fat include_____, _____, _____, and _____. (Note: could also include the following: adds visual appeal, moisture, aids in heat transfer, prevents items from sticking, creates tender texture or crisp texture.)

19. There are two kind of vitamins, _____ and _____. Both are found in _____.

Matching
Select the single best match for each item

_____ 20. Maillard reaction
_____ 21. Coagulation
_____ 22. Convection
_____ 23. Radiation
_____ 24. Evaporation
_____ 25. Caramelization

a. Transfer of heat through space
b. Browning of sugar caused by exposure to heat
c. An effect of protein denaturation
d. Transfer of heat through gases or liquids
e. Browning of protein and sugar caused by exposure to heat
f. Makes reduction possible

15

Essay/Short Answer
Answer each question as fully as possible

26. What is the importance of nutrition to the culinary professional?

_____

_____

_____

_____

_____

27. What is the importance of food science to the culinary professional?

_____

_____

_____

_____

_____

28. List and discuss the four sources of calories. For each, state the number of calories per gram, the percentage of daily calorie intake recommended by the USDA, and the primary functions.

_____

_____

_____

_____

_____

29. Describe the Maillard reaction.

_____

_____

_____

_____

_____

30. Describe conduction, convection, and radiation, explaining and giving examples of each.

_____

_____

_____

CHAPTER 4

Chapter Overview

The importance of food and kitchen safety cannot be overemphasized. Few things are as detrimental to a food service establishment as an officially noted outbreak of a food-borne illness caused by poor sanitary practices. In addition to providing a sanitary atmosphere and adhering to procedures for safe food handling, it is also important to ensure a safe working environment by reducing or eliminating any potential causes of injury to staff.

Chapter Objectives

After reading and studying this chapter, you will be able to:

➢ Explain what is meant by adulterated foods and the ways in which foods become adulterated

➢ Name the types of pathogens responsible for food-borne illness, and describe how they affect foods as well as how they reproduce in foods

➢ Name and explain the three conditions for pathogen growth in potentially hazardous foods

➢ List and use several techniques to avoid cross contamination

➢ Explain the importance of proper hand washing

➢ Keep foods out of the danger zone

➢ Hold, cool, reheat, and serve cooked or ready-to-serve foods safely

➢ Thaw frozen foods safely

➢ Explain what is meant by Hazard Analysis Critical Control Points (HACCP) and describe the use of a HACCP plan in a professional kitchen

➢ Explain what is meant by kitchen safety and list several guidelines and techniques for maintaining safety in the kitchen and dining room

➢ Identify the appropriate regulations, inspections, and certifications required of foodservice personnel

Study Outline

Food-borne Illness

Key Terms and Concepts

adulterated foods	biological contaminant	chemical contaminant
food-borne illness	infection	intoxication
microorganism	pathogen	physical contaminant

Food Pathogens

Key Terms and Concepts

aerobic bacteria
bacteria
fungi
virus

anaerobic bacteria
endospore
parasite

Aw scale
facultative bacteria
pH scale

Avoiding Cross Contamination

Key Terms and Concepts

cross contamination

personal hygiene

unsanitary handling procedures

Keeping Foods out of the Danger Zone

Key Terms and Concepts

danger zone
four-hour period
time and temperature control

dry storage
refrigeration

FIFO
thermometer

Hold Cooked or Ready-to-Serve Foods Safely

Key Terms and Concepts

cold-holding equipment

hot-holding equipment

hot foods hot, cold foods cold

Cooling Foods Safely

Key Terms and Concepts

ice-water bath

improperly cooled food

two-stage cooling method

Reheating Foods Safely

Key Terms and Concepts

direct heat
steam table

instant-read thermometer

reheating

Thawing Frozen Foods Safely

Key Terms and Concepts

microwave
running water

refrigeration
thaw

room temperature

Hazard Analysis Critical Control Point (HACCP)

Key Terms and Concepts

assessment	corrective action	critical control point
critical limit	hazard	record-keeping
verification		

Cleaning and Sanitizing

Key Terms and Concepts

air-dry	cleaning	sanitizing
soil	sanitizing solution	three-compartment sink
ware-washing machine		

Kitchen Safety

Key Terms and Concepts

accident	good general health	fire dangers
fire extinguisher	fire safety plan	protective uniforms
sanitize		

Regulations, Inspection, and Certification

Key Terms and Concepts

accessibility	Americans with Disabilities	local jurisdiction
Occupational Safety and Health	Act (ADA)	
Administration (OSHA)	state jurisdiction	worker safety

Drugs and Alcohol in the Workplace

Key Terms and Concepts

alcohol	drugs	hazard
impair	influence	substance abuse

Chapter 4 Exercises

True/False

Indicate whether each of the following statements is True (T) or False (F)

_____1.   The microorganisms that cause food to spoil are different from the ones that cause food-borne illness.

_____2.   Food that contains pathogens in great enough numbers to cause illness may still look and smell normal.

19

____3.	The higher the amount of protein in a food, the greater its potential as a carrier of a food-borne illness.

____4.	Foods with a water activity above 0.35 support bacterial growth.

____5.	A high pH (between 12 and 14) is best for bacterial growth.

____6.	After sanitizing, equipment and tableware should be thoroughly dried with sterile toweling because air-drying could result in contamination.

____7.	In the chef's uniform, the apron is worn to protect the uniform from excessive staining and for wiping hands that might otherwise be wiped on a side towel.

____8.	Athletic shoes are ideal for working in a kitchen because they provide support when standing for several hours at a time.

____9.	If a ware-washing machine is not available, small equipment, tools, pots, and tableware may be washed manually in a three-compartment sink.

____10.	HACCP is a federally mandated program established and regulated by the FDA and USDA.

Multiple Choice

Circle the single best answer for each

11. When there is not time to thaw foods in the refrigerator, they may be wrapped and placed under running water at or below approximately
    a. 41°F/5°C.
    b. 70°F/21°C.
    b. 100°F/38°C.
    c. 140°F/60°C.

12. When keeping foods out of the danger zone, you must observe temperature and
    a. time.
    b. level of moisture.
    c. pH level.
    d. exposure to cross contamination.

13. Storing and arranging foods using the FIFO principle will allow you to
    a. avoid cross contamination
    b. always use the oldest items first.
    c. ensure that items are wrapped and labeled correctly.
    d. divide the storage space into units and avoid overcrowding.

14. HACCP guidelines are established in a restaurant primarily to
    a. prevent conditions responsible for food-borne illness.
    b. problem-solve in areas where safety problems have occurred.
    c. set up record-keeping systems established and required by FDA and USDA.
    d. establish safe handling procedures for cooking, holding, and reheating food.

15. If a potentially hazardous prepared food is held at an incorrect temperature for too long, it must be
    a. frozen before reheating.
    b. brought immediately to a temperature below or above the danger zone.
    c. brought to a temperature of at least 165°F/74°C.
    d. discarded.

Fill in the Blank

For each space, insert the most appropriate response

16. To avoid cross contamination, wiping cloths should be held in _____ near each work station.

17. The 1999 FDA Food Code states that hands should be washed with soap in _____ degree water for _____.

18. The expression "Keep hot foods hot and cold foods cold" refers to the fact that all hot foods should be held in hot-holding equipment at _____ degrees or higher. Cold items should be held no warmer than _____ degrees.

19. The maximum amount of time foods may remain in the danger zone is _____.

20. The amount of moisture available in a food is measured on the _____ scale.

Matching

Select the single best match for each item

_____ 21. HACCP	a. measure of the amount of moisture present
_____ 22. bacteria	b. temperature range most suitable for the growth of microorganisms
_____ 23. danger zone	c. agency responsible for helping maintain safe, healthy work environments
_____ 24. Aw scale	d. agency responsible for making public places accessible and safe for those with disabilities
_____ 25. ADA	e. a system to recognize and prevent potentially hazardous conditions
_____ 26. OSHA	f. microorganisms

Essay/Short Answers
Answer each question as fully as possible

27. Discuss the personal responsibilities of the culinary professional in terms of food and kitchen safety, including personal hygiene, uniform, and behavior.

_____

_____

_____

_____

_____

_____

28. What is HACCP and what are its seven principles?

_____

_____

_____

_____

_____

_____

29. What are the components of a comprehensive fire safety plan?

_____

_____

_____

_____

_____

_____

30. What is the temperature danger zone? Why do foodservice professionals need to be aware of this?

_____

_____

_____

_____

_____

31. How should foods be received and stored?

_____

_____

_____

CHAPTER 5

EQUIPMENT IDENTIFICATION

Chapter Overview

Tools, large and small, are what make it possible for a chef to do the job properly, and using the correct tool for the job is one of the hallmarks of a professional. Equally important is the ability to handle and care for all tools, whether it be a cutting board, a knife, a mandoline, or a stockpot. Professional trade shows and journals allow culinarians to keep up with the latest equipment innovations and learn time- and labor-saving tricks and techniques.

Chapter Objectives

After reading and studying this chapter, you will be able to:

➢ Use the rules for knife care, use, and storage to perform all cutting tasks safely and efficiently

➢ Identify the basic parts of a knife

➢ Identify a variety of knives and their uses

➢ List a number of sharpening and honing tools and explain how to use sharpening and honing techniques to keep knives functioning safely and efficiently

➢ Name a variety of hand tools, describe their function, and select and use these tools properly to complete a specific task

➢ Name a variety of small equipment, including measuring equipment, sieves, and strainers

➢ Identify large equipment used to grind, slice, mix, and purée foods

➢ List the guidelines for working safely with large equipment

➢ Name and describe a variety of kettles, steamers, ranges, and ovens

➢ Name and describe various types of refrigeration equipment

Study Outline

The Parts of a Knife

Key Terms and Concepts

bolster	carbon steel	handle
high-carbon stainless steel	hollow-ground	rat-tail
rivet	rosewood	stainless steel
tang	taper-ground	

Types of Knives

Key Terms and Concepts

boning knife	chef's knife	cleaver
filleting knife	French knife	paring knife
slicer	tourné knife	utility knife

Sharpening and Honing

Key Terms and Concepts

Arkansas stone	carborundum stone	diamond-impregnated stone
grit	lubricant	sharpening stone

Steels

Key Terms and Concepts

ceramic	diamond steel	glass
guard	stroke	

Hand Tools

Key Terms and Concepts

kitchen fork	offset spatula	palette knife
Parisienne scoop	rolling pin	rotary peeler
whip/whisk		

Measuring Equipment

Key Terms and Concepts

balance-beam scale	candy/deep-fat thermometer	electronic scale
instant-read thermometer	measuring pitcher	measuring spoon
probe thermometer	spring scale	

Sieves and Strainers

Key Terms and Concepts

cheesecloth	colander	conical sieve
drum sieve	food mill	ricer
sieve	strainer	

Kettles and Steamers

Key Terms and Concepts

convection steamer	deep-fat fryer	pressure steamer
steam-jacketed kettle	tilting kettle	

Ranges and Ovens

Key Terms and Concepts

combi oven	convection oven	conventional/deck oven
flattop range	induction cooktop	microwave oven
open-burner range	ring-top range	

Griddles and Grills

Key Terms and Concepts

broiler	griddle	grill
salamander		

Grinding, Slicing, Mixing, and Puréeing Equipment

Key Terms and Concepts

blender	buffalo chopper	food chopper
food processor	food slicer	immersion blender
mandoline	meat grinder	standing mixer
vertical chopping machine		

Refrigeration Equipment

Key Terms and Concepts

display refrigeration	on-site refrigeration	portable refrigeration
reach-in	walk-in	

Chapter 5 Exercises

True/False

Indicate whether each of the following statements is True (T) or False (F)

_____ 1.   Rat-tail tangs are preferable to full tangs in knives that will be used frequently.

_____ 2.   The duller the blade, the finer the grit should be to ensure that the knife will be sharpened properly.

_____ 3.   Sieves and strainers are used to sift, aerate, and remove large impurities from dry ingredients.

_____ 4. Immersion blenders and burr mixers are ideal when puréeing a sauce directly in its cooking vessel.

_____ 5. Because pressure does not build up in the cooking unit of a convection steamer, the door to the unit may be opened at any time without danger of scalding or burning.

_____ 6. When straining or draining hot liquids, the drum sieve would be the best choice of strainers.

_____ 7. After use, rolling pins should be carefully washed with clean hot water and thoroughly dried.

_____ 8. It is possible to zone a walk-in to maintain appropriate temperature and humidity levels for storing various foods.

_____ 9. In a pressure steamer, water is heated under pressure in a sealed compartment, allowing it to reach temperatures above 212°F/100°C.

_____ 10. If a blade requires more than five strokes per side on a steel, it probably should be sharpened on a stone.

Multiple Choice

Circle the single best answer for each

11. When preparing large quantities of sautéed vegetables, the best equipment would be
    a. steam-jacketed kettle.
    b. tilting kettle.
    c. pressure steamer.
    d. combi oven.

12. When preparing a large quantity of stock, the best equipment would be
    a. steam-jacketed kettle.
    b. tilting kettle.
    c. pressure steamer.
    d. combi oven.

13. At breakfast service, when preparing large quantities of eggs, the best equipment would be
    a. omelet pans.
    b. sauteuse.
    c. flattop.
    d. frying pan.

14. To extend the life of a rolling pin, it should always be cleaned with
    a. a paper towel and salt.
    b. a dry cloth.
    c. a double-strength sanitizing solution.
    d. clean hot water.

15. When sharpening on a stone, the blade of the knife should always be passed
    a. tip to heel each time.
    b. heel to tip each time.
    c. horizontally.
    d. in the same direction each time.

Fill in the Blank
For each space, insert the most appropriate response

16. The Parisienne scoop is specifically designed for _____.

17. When using a stone to sharpen a knife, the lubricants of choice would be _____ or _____.

18. Three types of stone used for sharpening knives are _____, _____, and _____.

19. Three non-electrical kitchen tools used to purée foods are _____, _____, and _____.

20. Three pieces of equipment that might be used in a professional kitchen to steam foods are _____, _____, and _____.

Matching
Select the single best match for each item

_____ 21. Tang   a. Oven in which the heat source lies underneath

_____ 22. Salamander   b. A continuation of the blade that extends into the knife's handle

_____ 23. Combi oven   c. Small broiler used primarily to finish or glaze foods

_____ 24. Deck oven   d. Knife with a curved blade

_____ 25. Mandoline   e. Both a steamer and a convection oven

_____ 26. Tourné   f. Slicing device

Essay/Short Answer
Answer each question as fully as possible

27. List the rules for knife care, use, and storage.

_____

_____

_____

_____

28. List and describe the eight knives discussed in the text and give examples of how each should be used.

_____

_____

_____

_____

_____

29. Explain the five guidelines of using a steel.

_____

_____

_____

_____

_____

30. What are the six safety precautions that must always be used when working with large equipment?

_____

_____

_____

_____

_____

31. Describe the five types of refrigeration discussed in the text.

_____

_____

_____

_____

_____

CHAPTER 6

MEAT, POULTRY, AND GAME IDENTIFICATION

Chapter Overview

For most restaurants, the purchase, preparation, and service of meats is one of the most expensive areas of the business – but also one of the most potentially profitable. In order to get the most value out of the meats purchased, it is important to understand how to select the right cut for a particular cooking method.

Chapter Objectives

After reading and studying this chapter, you will be able to

➤ Explain basic meat concepts such as inspection, grading, and storage of beef, veal, pork, lamb, and poultry

➤ Explain the difference between meat inspection and quality grading

➤ Identify a variety of cuts for each type of meat and game

➤ Identify a variety of types of poultry and game birds

➤ Pair specific cuts of meat or poultry with the appropriate cooking method(s)

Study Outline

Meat Basics

Key Terms and Concepts

freshness	Meat Buyer's Guide	NAMP
wholesomeness		

Inspection and Grading

Key Terms and Concepts

antemortem	carcass	cutability
inspection	postmortem	quality grading
slaughterhouse	yield grade	

Market Forms of Meat

Key Terms and Concepts

boxed meat	food service cut	HRI cut

| portion control cut | primal cut | saddle |
| side | subprimal | value added cut |

Kosher Meats

Key Terms and Concepts

| dietary laws | kosher meat | shohet |

Beef

Key Terms and Concepts

beef	bovine	brisket
canner	choice	chuck
commercial	cutter	flank
foreshank	heifer	loin
offal	plate	prime
rib	round	select
short loin	sirloin	standard
steer	utility	variety meat

Veal

Key Terms and Concepts

breast	calf	choice
cull	foresaddle	foreshank
formula-fed	good	hindsaddle
hotel rack	leg	loin
milk-fed	offal	prime
square-cut shoulder	standard	utility
variety meat	veal	

Pork

Key Terms and Concepts

belly	Boston butt	fatback
foot	ham	hock
jowl	loin	offal
picnic	pig	pork
spare ribs	swine	USDA 1-4
variety meat		

Lamb and Mutton

Key Terms and Concepts

breast	chined	choice
chuck	cull	foresaddle
foreshank	good	grain-finished
grass-fed	hindsaddle	hotel rack
lamb	leg	loin
milk-fed	mutton	offal
prime	sheep	shoulder
utility	variety meat	

Venison and Furred Game

Key Terms and Concepts

buffalo	domesticated	free-roaming
game	hare	large game
quality	rabbit	small game
venison	wild boar	

Poultry

Key Terms and Concepts

age	broiler	capon
chicken	duck	foie gras
fowl	fryer	goose
guinea hen	pheasant	pigeon
poultry	poussin	quail
roaster	Rock Cornish hen	squab
turkey	USDA A-C	

Chapter 6 Exercises

True/False

Indicate whether each of the following statements is True (T) or False (F)

_____ 1. Both inspection and quality grading are mandatory for all meats slaughtered in the United States.

_____ 2. Beef from the chuck is best suited for roasting and grilling.

_____ 3. Once unwrapped, meats should be rewrapped in air-permeable paper to prevent bacterial growth and spoilage.

_____ 4. Once a spring lamb begins to eat grass or grain, its flesh loses its delicate, fine texture.

_____ 5. When selecting a meat item to be grilled or sautéed, you should choose an extremely tender cut.

_____ 6. The *Meat Buyer's Guide*, published by the National Association of Meat Purveyors, lists the appropriate price range for each cut of meat for the following six months.

_____ 7. The USDA inspection stamp should be present on any pork cut purchased from a reputable purveyor.

_____ 8. In veal, the shank is part of the leg primal cut.

_____ 9. Fryer chickens are both older and heavier than broiler chickens.

_____ 10. States may choose to administer their own inspections of meat provided they meet or exceed federal standards.

Multiple Choice

Circle the single best answer for each

11. When preparing braised veal, a suitable cut comes from the
    a. organs.
    b. shank.
    c. rack.
    d. loin.

12. The most common cooking methods for cuts from the beef loin are
    a. moist heat cooking methods.
    b. dry heat cooking methods.
    c. combination cooking methods.
    d. any method.

13. Boston butt is a regional name given to pork cuts from the
    a. shoulder.
    b. rib.
    c. loin.
    d. leg.

14. Ham steaks are generally cut from the
    a. shoulder.
    b. rib.
    c. loin.
    d. leg.

15. The primal cuts for veal are
   a. shoulder, ham, ribs, and breast.
   b. shoulder, shank, breast, and leg.
   c. shoulder, rack, loin, and leg.
   d. shoulder, shank, round, loin, and leg.

Fill in the Blank

For each space, insert the most appropriate response

16. _____ are only butchered from animals that have been slaughtered by a _____ _____, or specially-trained rabbi.

17. Some menu terms used in conjunction with cuts from beef tenderloin include

   _____, _____, _____,

   and _____.

18. Organ meats are also referred to as _____ or _____ meats.

19. Meat chops are most often fabricated from the _____ or _____ primal cuts.

20. All meats must be inspected according to federal standards before slaughter, called _____, and after butchering, called _____.

Matching

Select the single best match for each item

_____ 21. Capon   a. Buddhist duck with the head removed

_____ 22. Chuck   b. 6 to 8 weeks old

_____ 23. Round   c. Meat from the hindquarter

_____ 24. Cutability   d. Meat from the forequarter

_____ 25. Pekin duck e. Castrated rooster

_____ 26. Quail   f. Yield grade

Essay/Short Answer

Answer each question as fully as possible

27. How should meat be properly stored? Explain fully.

_____

_____

_____

_____

28. Explain the differences among inspection, quality grading, and yield grading and why this information is important to a chef.

_____

_____

_____

_____

_____

29. List the beef primal cuts and give two examples of cuts from each, along with appropriate cooking methods.

_____

_____

_____

_____

_____

30. Describe the meat of venison and rabbit.

_____

_____

_____

_____

_____

31. What is the major physical difference between beef and veal? How do the grades differ? Why are there fewer cuts of veal than of beef?

_____

_____

_____

_____

_____

CHAPTER 7

Chapter Overview

As fish and shellfish have become more and more popular, many familiar varieties are increasingly difficult to obtain as demand outstrips supply; therefore, many lesser-known fish and shellfish are becoming available. The increased value of seafood demands that a chef be familiar with a wide variety of fish and shellfish to address consumers' needs.

Chapter Objectives

After reading and studying this chapter, you will be able to:

➢ Name the basic market forms for flat and round fish and shellfish

➢ Identify a number of fish and categorize them (flat or round, bony and nonbony, activity levels)

➢ Pair specific fish with the appropriate cooking method(s)

➢ Handle fish and shellfish safely during storage and preparation

➢ Name the basic guidelines for purchasing fish and shellfish

➢ Identify a number of shellfish and categorize them (mollusk, crustacean, cephalopod)

➢ Pair specific shellfish with the appropriate cooking method(s)

Study Outline

Market Forms of Fish

Key Terms and Concepts

drawn	dressed	fillet
H&G	head-off drawn	pavé
steak	tranche	whole

Freshness Checks for Finfish

Key Terms and Concepts

40°F/4°C	belly burn	mucous
scales		

Common Fish Types

Key Terms and Concepts

activity level
caudal fin
gill plate
pectoral fin
rib

anal fin
dorsal fin
nonbony
pelvic fin
round

backbone
flat
oil content
pinbone
vent

Flat Fish

Key Terms and Concepts

continuous fin
gray sole/witch flounder
lemon sole
pigmented
right-eyed
winter/black-back flounder/
    mud dab

Dover sole
halibut
non-pigmented
plaice/rough dab
rock sole
yellowtail flounder

fluke/summer flounder
left-eyed
petrale/petrale sole
rex sole
turbot

Low-Activity Round Fish

Key Terms and Concepts

cod
pollock

haddock
white hake

low-activity
wolf fish

Medium-Activity Round Fish

Key Terms and Concepts

black grouper
hybrid bass/hybrid striped bass
red snapper
tilefish
weakfish

black sea bass
medium-activity
silk snapper
vermillion snapper/beeliner/
    Caribeau snapper

gag grouper
red grouper
striped bass
walleyed pike
yellowtail snapper

High-Activity Round Fish

Key Terms and Concepts

albacore tuna/tombo tuna
Atlantic salmon
bluefish
greater amberjack
king/Pacific salmon
permit
shad
Spanish mackerel

Arctic char
bigeye tuna/ahi-B
brook trout
high-activity
lesser amberjack
pompano
skipjack tuna/aku
steelhead trout

Atlantic mackerel
bluefin tuna
coho/silver salmon
king mackerel
mahi mahi/dolphin fish
rainbow trout
sockeye/red salmon
yellowfin tuna/ahi

Nonbony Fish

Key Terms and Concepts

cartilaginous
monkfish
swordfish

dogfish /Cape shark
skate/ray
thresher shark

mako shark
sturgeon

Other Fish

Key Terms and Concepts

American catfish
John Dory
wolf fish/ocean catfish

anchovy
sardine

eel
tilapia/mud fish

Shellfish

Key Terms and Concepts

bivalve
mollusk

cephalopod
univalve

crustacean

Market Forms

Key Terms and Concepts

liquor

shucked

shucking

Molluskan Shellfish

Key Terms and Concepts

abalone
calico scallop
conch
geoduck clam
land snail/escargot
periwinkle
razor/Atlantic jackknife clam
soft-shelled/Ipswich/horse
      clam/steamer

bay/Cape Cod/Long Island
      scallop
East Coast oyster
green mussel
Manila/West Coast littleneck
      clam
sea scallop/diver scallop
whelk/channel whelk

blue mussel
cockle
European flat oyster
Japanese/West Coast oyster
Pacific/Olympia oyster
quahog clam
sea urchin/uni

Cephalopods

Key Terms and Concepts

cuttlefish

octopus

squid/calamari

Crustacean Shellfish

Key Terms and Concepts

blue crab
Dungeness crab
king/Alaska king crab
rock shrimp
snow crab
tiger shrimp

cold water shrimp
freshwater shrimp
langoustine/Dublin Bay
    prawn/scampi
soft-shell crab
warm water shrimp

crayfish/crawfish
Jonah crab
Maine/northern/North
    American lobster
spiny/rock lobster

Chapter 7 Exercises

True/False

Indicate whether each of the following statements is True (T) or False (F)

_____ 1. For commercial culinary purposes, a whole fish is a fish with the viscera removed, but the head, tail, and fins are still intact.

_____ 2. Fish should be received at a temperature of 35°F/3°C or less

_____ 3.   Skate is a type of nonbony fish. The portions of the skate that are eaten are the wings.

_____ 4. Ice glazing is a technique for preserving fish fillets.

_____ 5. The more a fish swims, the paler and less oily its flesh will be.

_____ 6. While low-activity and high-activity fish are quite versatile, only a few cooking techniques are appropriate for medium-activity fish.

_____ 7. One sign of freshness and quality in fish is gill color, which should be a pale pink.

_____ 8. Shucking is the removal of a mollusk from its shell.

_____ 9. Belly burn occurs when bacteria and enzymes break down the flesh along the fish's ribs.

_____ 10. Crustaceans are mollusks with tentacles attached directly to the head.

Multiple Choice

Circle the single best answer for each

11. Which of these is a bivalve?

    a. conch.
    b. whelk.
    c. periwinkle.
    d. cockle.

12. Haddock is a member of which family?

    a. sea bass.
    b. flounder.
    c. mackerel.
    d. cod.

13. Which of these is a high-activity round fish?

    a. cod.
    b. red snapper.
    c. brook trout.
    d. turbot.

14. Which of these is a cephalopod?

    a. langoustine.
    b. octopus.
    c. warm water shrimp.
    d. turbot.

15. Which of the following is *not* a type of oyster discussed in the text?

    a. cockle.
    b. horse's hoof.
    c. East Coast oyster.
    d. West Coast oyster.

Fill in the Blank

For each space, insert the most appropriate response

16. A _____ has a backbone along the upper edge with two fillets on either side. A __ _____ has a backbone that runs through the center of the fish, with four fillets, two upper and two lower.

17. Three types of scallops available commercially are _____, _____, and _____.

18. Besides cod, three members of the cod family described in the text are _____, _____ _____, and _____.

19. Skate is a type of _____ fish. The portion of the skate that is eaten is the _____.

20. Besides shark, four types of nonbony fish mentioned in the text are _____, _____, _____, and _____. These fish have _____ rather than bones.

Matching
Select the single best match for each item

_____ 21. Crustacean	a. Snail
_____ 22. Steak	b. Cross-cut portion of a dressed fish
_____ 23. Escargot	c. Fish with guts, scales, fins, and perhaps head and tail removed
_____ 24. Tranche	d. Univalve with a suction cup that attaches to rocks
_____ 25. Dressed	e. Shellfish with exterior jointed skeletons or shells
_____ 26. Abalone	f. Portion of a fillet cut at a 45-degree angle

Essay/Short Answer
Answer each question as fully as possible

27. List and describe 8 market forms of fish.

_____

_____

_____

_____

_____

_____

28. List the six steps for proper storage and handling of fish.

_____

_____

_____

_____

_____

29. Define shellfish and describe the four general categories of shellfish.

_____

_____

_____

_____

_____

30. Discuss two methods of categorizing fish and the characteristics of each category within each method.

_____

_____

_____

_____

_____

_____

31. What are the quality indicators for selecting live shellfish?

_____

_____

_____

_____

_____

_____

CHAPTER 8

Chapter Overview

Fruits, vegetables, and herbs have always been an important part of the human diet, but today consumers are more aware than ever of the important role these foods play in maintaining overall health and fitness. This chapter provides professional chefs with the information they need to take full advantage of the abundance of fresh produce now available, including tips on availability, determination of quality, proper storage, and culinary usage.

Chapter Objectives

After reading and studying this chapter, you will be able to

➢ List the general guidelines for selecting fresh fruits, vegetables, and herbs

➢ Describe common agricultural methods and technologies and the advantages of each

➢ Discuss seasonality and its relevance to the contemporary chef

➢ Name the basic procedures for storing fresh produce

➢ Identify and name quality factors for a variety of fresh fruits, vegetables, and herbs

➢ Name the general categories for fruits and vegetables

Study Outline

Production Methods

Key Terms and Concepts

biotechnology	cold pasteurization	genetic engineering
genetically modified organism	hydroponics	irradiation
organic	sustainable agriculture	

Storage

Key Terms and Concepts

ethylene gas	overripe	ripening
spoilage		

Fruits

Key Terms and Concepts

dried fruit	fruit	ovary
seeds		

Vegetables

Key Terms and Concepts

botanical fruit	culinary application	flower head
leaf	leaf stalk	root
seed	seedpod	stem
tuber		

Herbs

Key Terms and Concepts

aroma	aromatic plants	dried
fresh		

Apples

Key Terms and Concepts

acidulate	browning	Cameo
Cortland	Cox Orange Pippin	crabapple
Gala	Golden Delicious	Granny Smith
Honey Crisp	McIntosh	Northern Spy
Red Delicious	Rome Beauty	Stayman Winesap

Berries

Key Terms and Concepts

blackberry	blueberry	cranberry
currant	gooseberry	perishable
raspberry	strawberry	

Citrus Fruits

Key Terms and Concepts

Aromatic oil	segmented flesh	blood orange
grapefruit	Key lime	lemon
lime	Mandarin orange	Meyer lemon
navel orange	Persian lime	Seville orange
tangelo	tangerine	Uniq™/Ugli fruit™

Grapes

Key Terms and Concepts

black	Black Corinth	Champagne
Concord	currant	raisin
Red Emperor	Thompson seedless	

Melons

Key Terms and Concepts

cantaloupe	casaba	Crenshaw
full slip	gourd	honeydew
muskmelon	Persian melon	watermelon

Pears

Key Terms and Concepts

acidulate	Asian pear	Bartlett/William
Bosc	browning	D'Anjou
Forelle	Seckel	

Stone Fruits

Key Terms and Concepts

apricot	cherry	Italian plum
nectarine	peach	pit
plum	stone	

Other Fruits

Key Terms and Concepts

avocado	banana	coconut
fig	guava	kiwifruit
mango	papaya	passion fruit
persimmon	pineapple	plantain
pomegranate	quince	rhubarb
starfruit	temperate	tropical

Cabbage

Key Terms and Concepts

Aspiration™/Broccolini™	baby bok choy/pak choy	bok choy/Chinese white cabbage
brassica	broccoli	broccoli rabe/rapini
Brussels sprouts	cauliflower	collard greens
green cabbage	heading cabbage	kale

kohlrabi/cabbage turnip   Napa/Chinese cabbage   red cabbage
Savoy cabbage   turnip greens

Soft-Shell Squash, Cucumber, and Eggplant

Key Terms and Concepts

chayote/mirliton	crookneck squash	cucumber
eggplant	English/burpless/hothouse/	gourd
immature	seedless cucumber	Japanese eggplant
Kirby cucumber	pattypan squash	soft-shell squash
squash blossom	standard/purple eggplant	standard/slicing cucumber
white eggplant	yellow squash	zucchini

Hard-Shell Squash

Key Terms and Concepts

acorn squash	butternut squash	delicate/sweet potato squash
gourd	Hubbard squash	pumpkin
rind	spaghetti squash	

Lettuce

Key Terms and Concepts

Bibb lettuce	Boston lettuce	butterhead
crisphead	green leaf lettuce	iceberg lettuce
leaf	oak leaf lettuce	red leaf lettuce
romaine	salad spinner	

Bitter Salad Greens

Key Terms and Concepts

arugula/rocket	Belgian endive	cooking methods
escarole	frisée	mâche/lamb's lettuce
radicchio	watercress	

Cooking Greens

Key Terms and Concepts

beet greens	cabbage family	cooking methods
dandelion greens	fibrous	mustard greens
spinach	Swiss chard	

Mushrooms

Key Terms and Concepts

cap
cremini
fungus
maitake/hen-of-the-woods
oyster
truffle

cèpe/porcini
cultivated
gills
matsutaki
portobello
white

chanterelle
enoki
lobster
morel
shiitake
wild

Onion Family

Key Terms and Concepts

boiling onion
dry
globe onion
pearl/creamer
shallot

cipollini
fresh
green
ramp/wild leek
Spanish/jumbo onion

cured
garlic
leek
scallion/green onion
sweet onion

Peppers

Key Terms and Concepts

Anaheim/California
chile/hot pepper
hot
mild
sweet pepper

bell pepper
Fresno
jalapeño
poblano

capsaicin
habanero
manzana
serrano

Pod and Seed Vegetables

Key Terms and Concepts

beans
cranberry bean
fava bean
haricot vert/French
   green bean
snow pea

Chinese long bean/yard-
   long bean
green bean
legume
pea
sugar snap pea

corn
edamame/green soy bean
green/English/garden pea
lima bean
Romano bean

Root Vegetables

Key Terms and Concepts

carrot
lotus root
purple-topped/white turnip
rutabaga/yellow turnip
turnip

celery root
malanga
radish
salsify/oyster plant

daikon
parsnip
root
standard beet

Tubers

Key Terms and Concepts

boniato
fingerling potato
jícama
russet/baking/Idaho potato
size C
tuber

cassava/yucca/manioc
galangal
purple potato
size A
sunchoke/Jerusalem artichoke
white potato

chef potato
ginger
red potato
size B
sweet potato/yam
yellow potato

Shoots and Stalks

Key Terms and Concepts

artichoke
fennel

asparagus
fiddlehead fern

celery

Tomatoes

Key Terms and Concepts

cherry tomato
heirloom tomato
plum/Italian plum/
    Roma tomato

commercially grown
locally grown
tomatillo

currant/cranberry tomato
pear tomato

Herbs

Key Terms and Concepts

basil
chive
dill
marjoram
parsley
savory

bay/laurel leaf
cilantro/Chinese parsley/
    coriander
mint
rosemary
tarragon

chervil
curry leaf
lemongrass
oregano
sage
thyme

Chapter 8 Exercises

True/False

Indicate whether each of the following statements is True (T) or False (F)

_____ 1.   Kirby cucumbers make excellent pickles.

_____ 2.   The term "stone fruit" refers to all fruit that has seeds or stones.

_____ 3. A quince is fruit with a flavor similar to oranges.

_____ 4. Unlike many other fruits, pears do not ripen after they are picked.

_____ 5. One advantage to using local growers is that boutique farmers may have specialty produce not available through commercial purveyors.

_____ 6. Tomatoes should never be refrigerated, because the cold makes their texture mushy, seizes their flavor, and halts ripening.

_____ 7. Generally, hydroponically-grown fruits and vegetables are preferable because they have a more pronounced flavor than soil-grown items.

_____ 8. For maximum flavor development, fresh herbs should be added early in the cooking process.

_____ 9. "Cipollini" is another name for "boiling onion."

_____ 10. Artichokes may be regionally known as Jerusalem artichokes or sunchokes.

Multiple Choice

Circle the single best answer for each

11. Because its flesh stays white after cutting longer than other varieties, a good choice of apple for fresh fruit salad would be
    a. Greening apples.
    b. Northern Spy apples.
    c. Golden Delicious apples.
    d. Crabapples.

12. Which of the following is a variety of cooking green?
    a. carrot greens.
    b. Swiss chard.
    c. Boston.
    d. Oakleaf.

13. Which of the following is *not* a component of fines herbes?
    a. thyme.
    b. chervil.
    c. tarragon.
    d. parsley.

14. The best type of orange for making orange marmalade or bigarade sauce would be
    a. Valencia.
    b. Seville.
    c. temple.
    d. Mandarin.

15. Which of the following is *not* a variety of soft-shell squash?
    a. Hubbard.
    b. Chayote.
    c. Crookneck.
    d. Yellow.

Fill in the Blank
For each space, insert the most appropriate response

16. Onions fall into two main categories, _____ and _____, which reflect the state in which they are used.

17. The major categories of greens are _____,_____, and

    _____.

18. Most produce should be kept at a temperature of _____ once it has ripened.

19. Fruits and vegetables that need further ripening, notably peaches and avocados, should be stored at a temperature of _____ until ripe.

20. Apples, bananas, and melons emit _____ gas which can accelerate

    _____ in other fruits.

Matching
Select the single best match for each item

_____ 21. Forelle		a. Long, thin cylinder with flat leaves
_____ 22. Crenshaw		b. Green or purple with brown papery husk
_____ 23. Red Emperor		c. Medium pear, golden with red blush and red speckles
_____ 24. Cipollini		d. Light to deep red grape with green streaking
_____ 25. Ramp		e. Honeydew-type muskmelon
_____ 26. Tomatillo		f. Small, flattened, round onion with yellow papery skin

Essay/Short Answer
Answer each question as fully as possible

27. In general, what constitutes good condition for fruits and vegetables?

_____

_____

_____

_____

_____

28. Why is purchasing local produce a favorable practice if and when possible?

_____

_____

_____

_____

_____

29. What are the five major members of the gourd family discussed in the text? Give two examples of each.

_____

_____

_____

_____

_____

30. List the six types of pears discussed in the text and give the common culinary uses of each.

_____

_____

_____

_____

_____

31. List the five types of shoot and stalk vegetables discussed in the text and give the common culinary uses of each.

_____

_____

_____

_____

_____

CHAPTER 9

DAIRY AND EGG PURCHASING AND IDENTIFICATION

Chapter Overview

A concentrated source of many nutrients, dairy products and eggs hold a prominent place on menus, on their own and as key ingredients in many preparations. Butter is a fundamental ingredient in numerous preparations, both as a cooking fat and as a flavoring. Milk, cream, crème fraîche, sour cream, and yogurt are used in sauces, salad dressings, and baked goods. Cheeses may be served as a separate course with fruit or as part of another dish. And eggs appear not just on their own, in breakfast dishes to dessert soufflés, but also in numerous sauces, especially emulsified ones such as hollandaise and mayonnaise.

Chapter Objectives

After reading and studying this chapter, you will be able to
➢ List the general guidelines for purchasing and storing dairy and eggs

➢ Explain what is meant by pasteurization and homogenization of liquid dairy

➢ Identify and describe a variety of dairy products

➢ Identify and describe a variety of fermented and cultured milk products

➢ Identify a variety of cheeses and group them according to milk type, texture, age, or ripening process

➢ Identify the parts of an egg and list several uses and functions for whole eggs, egg yolks, and egg whites

➢ Name the grades, sizes, and processed forms of eggs

Study Outline
Purchasing and Storage

Key Terms and Concepts

contamination	curdle	flavor transfer
freshness period	spoilage	

Milk

Key Terms and Concepts

condensed milk	dry milk	evaporated milk
Grade A	homogenized	milk
nonfat milk	pasteurized	powdered milk

| reduced-fat milk | skim milk | sour cream |
| ultrapasteurized | whole milk | yogurt |

Cream

Key Terms and Concepts

butterfat	centrifuge	cream
half-and-half	heavy cream	light cream
milkfat	stabilized	whipping cream

Ice Cream

Key Terms and Concepts

frozen dairy food	frozen yogurt	gelato
ice cream	ice milk	milk fat
rice milk frozen dessert	sherbet	sorbet
soy milk frozen dessert	stabilizers	vanilla
weeping		

Butter

Key Terms and Concepts

butter	buttermilk	churning
Grade A	Grade AA	Grade B
milk fat	overwhipping	salted butter
sweet butter	sweet cream	

Fermented and Cultured Milk Products

Key Terms and Concepts

| buttermilk | crème fraîche | culture |
| fermentation | sour cream | yogurt |

Cheese

Key Terms and Concepts

acid	blue-veined cheeses	buffalo's milk
cheese foods	cow's milk	curds
fresh cheeses	goat's milk	grating cheeses
hard cheeses	maturity	natural cheeses
overripening	pasteurized cheeses	processed cheeses
rennet	ripening	soft/rind-ripened cheeses
semisoft cheeses	sheep's milk	spoiling
starter	whey	

Fresh Cheeses

Key Terms and Concepts

Boursin	chèvre	cottage cheese
cream cheese	farmer's cheese	feta
fromage blanc	mascarpone	mozzarella
queso fresco	ricotta	

Soft/Rind-Ripened Cheeses

Key Terms and Concepts

Brie	Camembert	double cream
Epoisses	Explorateur	Limburger
Pont l'Évêque	Reblochon	single cream
surface mold	Taleggio	triple cream

Semisoft Cheeses

Key Terms and Concepts

Caciotta	dry-rind	Fontina
Havarti	Monterey Jack	Morbier
Muenster	Port-Salut	wash-rind
wax-rind		

Firm Cheeses

Key Terms and Concepts

Cantal	Cheddar	cheddaring
Emmentaler	Gouda	Gruyère
Jarlsberg	Manchego	Provolone
ricotta salata		

Hard Cheeses

Key Terms and Concepts

aging	Asiago	dry Monterey Jack
eating cheese	Grana Padano	Parmigiano-Reggiano
Pecorino Romano	Sap Sago	table cheese

Blue-Veined Cheeses

Key Terms and Concepts

Danish blue	Gorgonzola	injection
Maytag blue	mold	Point Reyes
ripening	Roquefort	Spanish blue
Stilton		

Grading, Sizes, and Forms

Key Terms and Concepts

bulk whole eggs	chalazae	dried eggs
egg substitute	extra large	fluid whole eggs
Grade AA	jumbo	large
medium	pasteurized eggs	peewee
small	whites	yolks

Chapter 9 Exercises
True/False

Indicate whether each of the following statements is True (T) or False (F).

_____ 1. The date stamped on milk that indicates how long the unopened milk will remain fresh is seven, ten, or sixteen days from the date the cow was milked.

_____ 2. When used in hot dishes, milk and/or cream should always be brought to a boil first to check for wholesomeness.

_____ 3. Some chefs prefer to use heavy cream that has been stabilized for whipping because they believe it will whip to greater volumes.

_____ 4. In most regions, half-and-half and light cream contain the same percentage of fat.

_____ 5. Most buttermilk sold today is nonfat milk that has been cultured.

_____ 6. The designation "sweet butter" indicates that no salt has been added to the butter during processing.

_____ 7. Crème fraîche is often preferred in cooking because it tends to curdle less readily than sour cream when used in hot dishes.

_____ 8. Processed or pasteurized cheeses and cheese foods do not ripen and their characteristics will not change.

_____ 9. Gorgonzola and Pont Reyes are categorized as grating cheeses.

_____ 10. Salted butter may contain no more than 2 percent of salt.

Multiple Choice

Circle the single best answer for each

11. Which of the following is _not_ a frozen dessert similar to ice cream?
    a. gelato.
    b. fromage blanc.
    c. sherbet.
    d. ice milk.

12. In order to meet government standards, the percentage of milkfat in heavy cream must be
    a. 36 percent.
    b. 34 percent.
    c. 50 percent.
    d. 18 percent.

13. Gruyère is
    a. a creamy fresh cheese.
    b. a soft cheese with an edible surface mold.
    c. a semi-soft cheese with a wax rind, good for slicing but not grating.
    d. a dryer firm cheese that slices and grates easily.

14. A good choice of cheese for slicing would be
    a. Jarlsberg.
    b. fromage blanc.
    c. Camembert.
    d. Gorgonzola.

15. A good cheese for grating would be
    a. mascarpone.
    b. Port Salut.
    c. Sap Sago.
    d. Roquefort.

Fill in the Blank

For each space, insert the most appropriate response

16. Low-fat and skim milk are almost always _____ because removing the fat removes many of the fat-soluble vitamins.

17. The appearance of "weeping" in melting ice cream indicates an excessive amount of

_____.

18. When cooking with milk or cream, the best way to check for spoilage before using is to

_____.

19. The date stamped on milk or cream that indicates how long the unopened milk will remain fresh is seven, ten, or sixteen days from the date the milk _____.

20. The percentage of fat in milk or cream is called the _____ or

_____.

Matching
Select the single best match for each item

_____ 21. Rennet	a. Percentage of fat in milk
_____ 22. Chalazae	b. Bacterial strain added to milk products
_____ 23. Butterfat	c. Membranes which anchor the yolk within the egg
_____ 24. Culture	d. Soft cheese made from whole or skim cow's or goat's milk
_____ 25. Fontina	e. Starter for cheese which causes milk to form curds
_____ 26. Brie	d. Semisoft cheese made from whole cow's or goat's milk

Essay/Short Answer
Answer each question as fully as possible

27. Discuss the processed forms of eggs, as discussed in the text.

_____
_____
_____
_____
_____
_____

28. How is butter made? What is salted butter, and why is it important? What is sweet butter? How is butter graded, and what are the qualities of each grade?

_____
_____
_____
_____
_____
_____

29. Explain the process through which most cheeses are made. What is the difference between natural and processed cheeses?

_____

_____

_____

_____

_____

_____

30. How do the ripening processes for soft/rind-ripened cheeses and semisoft cheeses differ?

_____

_____

_____

_____

_____

31. What are grating cheeses? Name three of the six discussed in the text and describe the culinary uses of each.

_____

_____

_____

_____

_____

_____

CHAPTER **10**

D**RY** G**OODS** I**DENTIFICATION**

Chapter Overview

A broad spectrum of dry goods forms part of any food service operation's basic needs. Whole grains, meals, and flours; dried legumes; dried pasta and noodles; nuts and seeds; sugars, syrups, and other sweeteners; oils and shortenings; vinegars and condiments; coffee, tea, and other beverages; dry goods for baking; dried herbs and spices; and cooking wines, liqueurs, and cordials must be chosen, purchased, and stored with the same degree of care as fresh meats or produce.

Dry goods such as these are occasionally referred to as nonperishable goods. However, these ingredients, like perishable goods, lose quality over time. Keeping an adequate parstock on hand is essential to a smooth running operation, but having too much ties up unnecessary space and money. Rotating dry goods and observing a rule of "first in, first out" is just as important for dry goods as for more perishable foods.

Chapter Objectives

After reading and studying this chapter, you will be able to:

➢ Describe general purchasing and storage guidelines for dry goods

➢ Discuss various forms of grains, giving examples of each along with their common culinary uses

➢ Explain the importance of dried pasta as a convenience food and describe a wide range of dried pastas and noodles, along with their common culinary uses

➢ Describe appropriate methods of purchasing, storing, and preparing dried legumes and identify a variety of dried legumes along with their common culinary uses

➢ Identify a number of nuts and seeds, together with their culinary uses and common purchasing forms

➢ Describe appropriate methods of purchasing, storing, and preparing dried spices and identify a variety of dried spices along with their common culinary uses

➢ Discuss the importance of salt and pepper, describing a number of forms and the common culinary uses of each

➢ Discuss some common sweeteners and their role in a kitchen, identifying a number of sugars and syrups and giving the common culinary uses of each

➢ Describe the uses of fats and oils in a kitchen and discuss a number of common fats and oils

➢ Use appropriate guidelines to select, use, prepare, and store coffee, tea, and other beverages; wines, cordials, and liqueurs; and a range of flavoring, thickening, and baking ingredients

Study Outline

Purchasing and Storage

Key Terms and Concepts

dry goods

first in, first out (FIFO)

nonperishable goods

Grains, Meals, and Flours

Key Terms and Concepts

all-purpose flour
amaranth
arborio rice
barley
basmati rice
bran
bread flour
brown rice
buckwheat
bulgur
cake flour
calaspara rice
cereal grasses
converted rice
corn
cornmeal
cornstarch
cracked wheat
durum flour
Ebly® wheat
farina
flour
germ
gluten
glutinous rice
grain
grits
groats
heirloom rice
hominy
Irish oats
Italian rice
jasmine rice
Job's tears
kasha
long-grain rice
masa
medium-grain rice
milled
millet
oat bran
oat flour
oats
old-fashioned oats
parboiled rice
pastry flour
pearl rice
polished
quinoa
rice
rolled oats
rye
Scotch oats
semolina
short-grain rice
sorghum
spelt
steel-cut oats
sticky rice
stone-ground
sushi rice
teff
tender wheat
wheat
wheat berries
white rice
whole grain
whole wheat
whole wheat flour
wild rice

Dried Pasta and Noodles

Key Terms and Concepts

acini di pepe
bucatini
bean thread noodles
capellini
casareccia
couscous
elbows
farfalle
fettuccine
Fregola Sarda
fusilli
Israeli couscous
Italian couscous
lasagna
linguine
noodle
orecchiette
orzo
pasta
penne
radiatore
rice noodles
rigatoni
shells
soba noodles
spaghetti
tubetti
udon noodles
vermicelli

Dried Legumes

Key Terms and Concepts

adzuki bean	bean	black bean
black-eyed pea	broad bean	butter bean
canary bean	cannellini bean	chickpea
cranberry bean	fava bean	flageolet
Gandules pea	garbanzo bean	Great Northern bean
Italian kidney bean	kidney bean	legume
lentil	lima bean	Mexican bean
mung bean	Navy bean	pea
pigeon pea	pinto bean	rice bean
soybean	split pea	turtle bean
Yankee bean		

Nuts and Seeds

Key Terms and Concepts

almond	Brazil nut	cashew
chestnut	filbert	flax seed
hazelnut	leguminous	macadamia
nut	peanut	pecan
pepita	pignoli	pine nut
pistachio	poppy seed	pumpkin seed
seed	sesame seed	sunflower seed
tree nut	walnut	

Dried Spices

Key Terms and Concepts

allspice	anardana	anise
annatto	aromatic	caraway
cardamom	cayenne	celery
chili powder	Chinese five-spice powder	cinnamon
clove	coriander	cumin
curry powder	dill	epazote
fennel	fenugreek	filé powder
garam masala	ginger	horseradish
juniper berry	mace	mustard
nutmeg	paprika	quatre épices
saffron	star anise	turmeric

Salt and Pepper

Key Terms and Concepts

anise pepper	bay salt	black peppercorn
canning salt	Chinese pepper	curing salt

green peppercorn
monosodium glutamate
pink peppercorn
sea salt
Szechwan peppercorn

iodized salt
peppercorn
rock salt
seasoned salt
table salt

kosher salt
pickling salt
salt substitute
sodium chloride
white peppercorn

Sweeteners

Key Terms and Concepts

10X sugar
caramelization
flavored syrup
jaggery
molasses
powdered sugar
sugarcane

artificial sweetener
confectioners' sugar
granulated sugar
maple sugar
palm sugar
raw sugar
syrup

brown sugar
corn syrup
honey
maple syrup
piloncilio
sugar
white sugar

Fats and Oils

Key Terms and Concepts

canola oil
corn oil
fat
grapeseed oil
oil spray
safflower oil
shortening
vegetable oil

clarified butter
cottonseed oil
frying fat
lard
olive oil
salad oil
soybean oil
walnut oil

coconut oil
drawn butter
ghee
oil
peanut oil
sesame oil
sunflower oil
whole butter

Chocolate

Key Terms and Concepts

bloom
cocoa beans
white chocolate

chocolate
cocoa butter

chocolate liquor
cocoa powder

Vinegars and Condiments

Key Terms and Concepts

condiment

vinegar

Extracts

Key Terms and Concepts

extract

flavoring

Leaveners

Key Terms and Concepts

baking powder   baking soda   chemical leavener
fermentation   yeast

Thickeners

Key Terms and Concepts

emulsion   thickener   viscosity

Coffee, Tea, and Other Beverages

Key Terms and Concepts

coffee   juice   preground
prepared mixes   tea   whole bean

Wines, Cordials, and Liqueurs

Key Terms and Concepts

cognac   cordial   fortified wine
liqueur   table wine   wine

Chapter 10 Exercises
True/False
Indicate whether each of the following statements is True (T) or False (F)

_____ 1. Nuts that have been shelled and roasted will keep longer than raw nuts.

_____ 2. Clarified butter has a longer shelf life than whole butter.

_____ 3. All chocolates contain some chocolate liquor, but white chocolate contains significantly less than milk or dark chocolate.

_____ 4. Rice is commercially classified by its gluten content.

_____ 5. Dark sesame oil has a low smoking point, so it is used primarily for flavoring rather than in cooking.

_____ 6. Sugar is extracted from plant sources, such as beets and sugarcane, and refined into the desired form.

_____ 7. Chocolate that develops a white "bloom" on its surface is probably rancid and should not be eaten.

_____ 8. Grains are the fruit and seeds of cereal grasses that provide a valuable source of nutrients and fiber.

_____ 9. Generally, grains that have been milled or polished are a better source of nutrients than whole grains.

_____ 10. Spices are aromatics produced primarily from the bark and seeds of plants.

Multiple Choice
Circle the single best answer for each

11. Farfalle are made from
    a. wheat flour.
    b. rice flour.
    c. mung bean starch.
    d. sweet potato starch.

12. Curing salts can be distinguished from other salts because they usually
    a. are marked "edible".
    b. have a gray tint.
    c. are dyed pink.
    d. are larger and more granular.

13. Soba noodles are made with
    a. wheat flour.
    b. rice flour.
    c. mung bean starch.
    d. buckwheat flour.

14. When choosing a fat or oil for deep-frying, you should select one that
    a. has been hydrogenated.
    b. has a high smoking point.
    c. has an appropriate flavor.
    d. is neutral in flavor.

15. Milled grains that are broken into coarse particles may be referred to as
    a. crushed.
    b. cracked.
    c. meal.
    d. flour.

Fill in the Blank

For each space, insert the most appropriate response

16. Nuts are the fruits of various _____, with the exception of the _____, which grows _____.

17. The benefit of purchasing milled grains rather than whole grains is that milled grains _____. The downside of milled grains is that they _____.

18. Depending on how coarsely or finely it is ground, cornmeal may be known as _____ or _____.

19. Good-quality dried pastas from wheat flour are customarily made from _____.

20. Three varieties of molasses are _____, _____, and _____.

Matching

Select the single best match for each item

_____ 21.	Paprika	a. Powder made from dried chile
_____ 22.	Grits	b. Powder made from dried sweet red peppers
_____ 23.	Bucatini	c. Dried kernels, cooked and soaked in limewater, then ground into dough
_____ 24.	Cayenne	d. Ground hominy
_____ 25.	Masa	e. Thick, ridged tubes
_____ 26.	Rigatoni	f. Hollow, long strands; spaghetti-shaped

Essay/Short Answer

Answer each question as fully as possible

27. Explain the proper storage procedures for dry goods.

_____

_____

_____

_____

_____

_____

28. What are grains? Whole grains? Milled grains?

_____

_____

_____

_____

_____

_____

29. What are legumes? How should they be purchased and prepared before cooking?

_____

_____

_____

_____

_____

_____

30. What are nuts? What are the common market forms? How should they be stored?

_____

_____

_____

_____

_____

_____

31. Describe the process of chocolate extraction.

_____

_____

_____

_____

_____

_____

CHAPTER 11

Chapter Overview

Good cooking is the result of carefully developing the best possible flavor and most perfect texture in each dish. It is therefore important to observe the basic principles of flavor development and thickening in each preparation. Basic flavoring and aromatic combinations constitute the flavor base; thickeners contribute a rich, smooth mouthfeel; and liaisons lend body to stocks, sauces, and soups.

Chapter Objectives

After reading and studying this chapter, you will be able to

➢ Define and use bouquet garni, sachet d'épices, and oignon brûlé, listing common ingredients for each and standard cooking times for flavor extraction

➢ Prepare mirepoix and be able to describe common ingredients and their handling and name several mirepoix variations

➢ Explain the uses for roux and name the basic colors of roux, express the basic ratio for roux as a weight, and combine roux and a liquid properly

➢ Prepare clarified butter and describe its appropriate or common uses

➢ Identify a variety of pure starches and their characteristics, use them to prepare a slurry, and substitute starches of different thickening powers in recipes using a standard formula

➢ Name the ingredients in a liaison, describe the effect of a liaison on a dish, and hold liaised dishes hot to preserve both wholesomeness and quality

Study Outline

Bouquets, Sachets, and Oignon Brûlé

Key Terms and Concepts

bouquet garni	loose sachet	oignon brûlé
oignon piqué	sachet d'épices	

Mirepoix

Key Terms and Concepts

aromatics	Asian aromatics	Cajun trinity

caramelized	edible mirepoix	matignon
mirepoix	pinçage	smothering
sweating	white mirepoix	

Roux

Key Terms and Concepts

3 to 2	blond roux	brown roux
dark roux	roux	"sand at low tide"
thickening power	white roux	

Clarified Butter

Key Terms and Concepts

clarified butter	clarify	decant
ghee	milk solids	water
whole butter		

Pure Starch Slurries

Key Terms and Concepts

arrowroot	cornstarch	potato starch
pure starch	rice flour	slurry
tapioca	thickening power	

Liaison

Key Terms and Concepts

| coagulation point | curdle | liaison tempering |

Chapter 11 Exercises

True/False

Indicate whether each of the following statements is True (T) or False (F)

_____ 1. A liaison is a modified starch dissolved in a cold liquid.

_____ 2. One pound of mirepoix is enough to flavor either 1 gallon of stock or 1 quart of sauce.

_____ 3. Roux is an essential ingredient in all soups.

_____ 4. When tempering a liaison, the egg yolks should never be added directly to the hot liquid.

_____ 5. Clarified butter is butter in which the milk solids have separated from the butterfat.

_____ 6. A basic formula for Asian aromatics is two parts ginger, two parts garlic, and one part green onion.

_____ 7. To substitute a pure starch for roux, multiply the weight of flour in roux by the thickening power of the replacement starch to obtain the estimated weight of the replacement starch desired.

_____ 8. An oignon brûlé is prepared by studding an onion with a few whole cloves and a bay leaf.

_____ 9. In a "loose" sachet, the sachet ingredients are added directly to the recipe without first being tied.

_____ 10. Dishes thickened with pure starch slurries tend to have exceptionally long holding periods.

Multiple Choice

Circle the single best answer for each

11. Sachet d'épices is a
    a. liaison.
    b. type of mirepoix.
    c. bundle of fresh herbs and vegetables.
    d. bag of spices usually containing parsley stems, thyme, bay leaf, and peppercorns.

12. For making a batch of stock that is several gallons or more, the bouquet garni is
    a. added about one hour before the end of the cooking time.
    b. commonly augmented with a sachet d'épices.
    c. added during the last fifteen to thirty minutes of cooking.
    d. commonly augmented with an oignon piqué.

13. Which of the following are part of the basic formula for matignon?
    a. Ham, onion, leek, thyme.
    b. Carrot, celery, onion, garlic.
    c. Onion, ham, carrot, celery.
    d. Thyme, celery, green bell pepper, onion.

14. Pinçage refers to
    a. the process of clarifying butter.
    b. the process of cooking tomato product with mirepoix until it becomes a rusty brown color.
    c. the proper addition of a liaison to a sauce.
    d. a method for making a pure starch slurry.

15. To thicken a liquid with a roux, add
    a. hot liquid to hot roux.
    b. cool liquid to hot roux.
    c. cool liquid to cool roux.
    d. temper hot liquid into cool roux, then add the roux mixture to the main hot liquid

Fill in the Blank
For each space, insert the most appropriate response

16. The purpose of clarifying butter is to remove _____ and _____.

17. Mirepoix is the French name for a combination of _____, _____, and _____.

18. The tempering process reduces _____ so that the finished soup or sauce remains _____.

19. A standard bouquet garni, adequate to flavor 1 gallon of liquid, includes _____, _____, _____, and 2 to 3 leek leaves and/or 1 celery stalk.

20. From lightest to darkest, the four basic colors of roux are _____, _____, _____, and _____.

Matching
Select the single best match for each item

_____ 21. Matignon   a. Method for cooking mirepoix uncovered until it releases liquid
_____ 22. Cajun trinity   b. Edible mirepoix; contains pork
_____ 23. Arrowroot   c. 0.5 thickening power; gels and weeps when cooled
_____ 24. Sweating   d. Onion, green bell pepper, celery
_____ 25. Cornstarch   e. Method for cooking mirepoix covered until it releases liquid
_____ 26. Smothering   f. 0.5 thickening power; does not gel or weep when cooled

Essay/Short Answer
Answer each question as fully as possible

27. List the basic formulas for mirepoix, white mirepoix, Asian aromatics, and Cajun trinity.

_____

_____

_____

_____

_____

28. What is the basic formula for a liaison, and what are the three steps in using a liaison in a sauce or soup?

_____

_____

_____

_____

_____

29. What is the basic formula for roux? How is it made? How are large quantities of roux kept from scorching?

_____

_____

_____

_____

_____

30. How should roux be combined with liquid? What are four guidelines to follow?

_____

_____

_____

_____

_____

31. Name five pure starches and describe the process for making and using a pure starch slurry.

_____

_____

_____

_____

_____

CHAPTER 12

Chapter Overview

Stocks are among the most basic preparations found in any professional kitchen. In fact, they are known in French as *fonds de cuisine*, or the foundations of cooking. A stock is a flavorful liquid prepared by simmering meaty bones from meat or poultry, seafood, and/or vegetables in water with aromatics until their flavor, aroma, color, body, and nutritive value are extracted. The liquid is then used to prepare sauces and soups and as a cooking medium for other recipes.

Chapter Objectives

After reading and studying this chapter, you will be able to
➢ Describe the characteristics and quality indicators for various stocks, fumets, and related preparations

➢ Prepare a variety of stocks, fumets, and related preparations

➢ Follow safe food handling practices for stocks

➢ Explain how to test and evaluate commercially prepared bases

Study Outline

Stocks

Key Terms and Concepts

aroma	body	brown stock
clarity	color	dépouiller
essence	evaporation rate	flavor
frémir	fumet	ratio
skim	stock	white stock

General Guidelines for Stocks

Key Terms and Concepts

commercial base	glace	glace de viande
reduction	remouillage	

Chapter 12 Exercises

True/False

Indicate whether each of the following statements is True (T) or False (F)

_____ 1. Fumets are sometimes known as essences.

_____ 2. Cold water slows the process of extracting flavor from the bones.

_____ 3. Pots used for stock are usually wider than they are tall.

_____ 4. The right time to add mirepoix to all stocks except court bouillons and fish stocks is about 2 hours before the end of cooking time.

_____ 5. Commercially-made bases are used only for institutional cooking, not for restaurant cooking.

_____ 6. The sachet d'épices should be added to the stock about 45 minutes before it has finished simmering.

_____ 7. Bones from older animals are generally preferred for making stock, as the bones will be larger.

_____ 8. The formula for one gallon of fish or shellfish stock is 8 pounds of bones and trimmings, 1.5 gallons of cool liquid, 1 pound mirepoix, and 1 standard sachet d'épices.

_____ 9. Stocks should never boil.

_____ 10. Quality brown stocks are a deep amber or brown due to the residual blood left in the finished product.

Multiple Choice

Circle the single best answer for each

11. The French name for a "secondary stock" is
    a. glace de viande.
    b. dépouiller.
    c. glace.
    d. remouillage.

12. An appropriate vessel for large-scale stock production is a
    a. steam-jacketed kettle.
    b. rondeau.
    c. tilting kettle.
    d. roasting pan.

13. Glaces are used

    a. instead of remouillage.

    b. to boost the flavor of other foods, especially sauces.

    c. to make remouillage.

    d. only when commercial bases are not available.

14. To make 1 gallon of brown stock, how much mirepoix is required?

    a. 8 ounces

    b. 24 ounces

    c. 16 ounces

    d. 20 ounces

15. Since fish stocks and fumets typically have brief cooking times, mirepoix for these preparations

    a. should be cut into large pieces.

    b. should be cut into small pieces.

    c. should be added near the end of the cooking process.

    d. should be puréed for maximum flavor extraction.

Fill in the Blank

For each space, insert the most appropriate response

16. Bones for stock should be cut into 3-inch lengths for quicker and more thorough extraction of _____, _____, and _____.

17. The French word _____, meaning _____, is used to describe the action of the bubbles as the stock cooks.

18. The _____ the stock, the _____ its shelf life.

19. Evaluate the quality of a finished stock on the basis of four criteria: _____, _____, _____, and _____.

20. Fumets are made by _____ or _____ the main ingredients before _____, often with the addition of a dry white wine.

Matching

Select the single best match for each item

_____ 21.	White mirepoix	a. Rubbery
_____ 22.	"Rewetting"	b. Essence
_____ 23.	Glace	c. An ingredient in fish stock
_____ 24.	White stock	d. Dépouiller
_____ 25.	Fumet	e. Clear and light to golden
_____ 26.	"To skin or peel"	f. Remouillage

Essay/Short Answer
Answer each question as fully as possible

27. What is the basic formula for brown or white stock? For fish or shellfish stock?

_____

_____

_____

_____

_____

_____

28. Discuss commercial bases – when they can be used, market forms, and quality evaluation.

_____

_____

_____

_____

_____

_____

29. What is a glace? What is it made from? How is it used?

_____

_____

_____

_____

_____

30. What gives a stock good flavor and body? Explain.

_____

_____

_____

_____

_____

31. What are the 6 steps in the procedure for making stock?

_____

_____

_____

_____

_____

_____

CHAPTER 13

Chapter Overview

Sauces are often considered one of the greatest tests of a chef's skill. The successful pairing of a sauce with a food demonstrates technical expertise, an understanding of the food, and the ability to judge and evaluate a dish's flavors, textures, and colors.

Chapter Objectives

After reading and studying this chapter, you will be able to

➤ Describe the characteristics and quality indicators for brown sauce, white sauce, tomato sauce, hollandaise, and beurre blanc

➤ Select and prepare the ingredients and equipment necessary to produce sauces

➤ Describe the correct method for producing various sauces

➤ List, describe, and identify uses for derivative sauces

➤ Prepare, hold, and reheat sauces for the best flavor, texture, and color

➤ Follow safe food handling practices for sauces

➤ Explain how and why sauces are combined with other foods

➤ Select sauces that are appropriate for specific foods, cooking techniques, or serving situations

Study Outline

Brown Sauce

Key Terms and Concepts

Bigarade	Bordelaise	Bourguignonne
Bretonne	brown sauce	brown stock
Charcutière	Chasseur/Huntsman's	Cherry
Chevreuil	demi-glace	Diane
espagnole	Financière	fortify
garnish	Genevoise/Génoise	Gratin
Italienne	jus de veau lié	Matelote
Mushroom	nappé	pan sauce
pincé	Poivrade	reduction sauce
reductions	Régence	Robert
thickener	Zingara	

White Sauce

Key Terms and Concepts

Albufera
Américaine
Aux Crevettes
Bohémienne
Cardinal
Diplomate
Huitres/Oyster
Sauce à l'Anglaise/Egg
thickener
Vin Blanc

Allemande/Parisienne
Aurore
béchamel
Bonnefoy
Chivry
Écossaise/Scotch Egg
Mornay
scorching
velouté
white sauce

aluminum
Aurore Maigre
Bercy
Bretonne
consistency
Homard à l'Anglaise/Lobster
Normande
Suprême
Villeroy

Tomato Sauce

Key Terms and Concepts

bitter
fresh
raw
thickener
weak

canned
harsh
Roma
tomato product

cooked
plum
sweet
tomato sauce

Hollandaise Sauce

Key Terms and Concepts

au sec
Béarnaise
Choron
emulsion
hollandaise sauce
melted whole butter
pasteurized egg yolk
Royal

acid
breaking
clarified butter
Foyot/Valois
hot-holding
Mousseline
reduction
salmonella

Bavaroise
butter
curdling
glaçage
Maltaise
Paloise
ribbons
"trails"

Beurre Blanc

Key Terms and Concepts

au sec
emulsion
nonreactive metal
stabilize

beurre blanc
hot-holding
reduction
whole butter

cuisson
monter au beurre
shallow-poach

The Purpose of Sauces

Key Terms and Concepts

complementary flavor   counterpoint flavor   moisture
succulence   texture   visual interest

Sauce Pairing

Key Terms and Concepts

balance   eye appeal   flavor of food
main ingredient   style of service   taste
texture

Guidelines for Plating Sauces

Key Terms and Concepts

balance   plate   portion size
temperature   texture of food visual appeal

Chapter 13 Exercises

True/False

Indicate whether each of the following statements is True (T) or False (F)

_____ 1. Classically, demi-glace is composed of equal parts espagnole and brown stock and is not reduced.

_____ 2. The thickener of choice for jus lié is arrowroot, because it results in a translucent, glossy sauce.

_____ 3. A roux-thickened brown sauce is opaque with a thick body.

_____ 4. To avoid scorching, white sauces should never be cooked enough to coat the back of a spoon.

_____ 5. An overly sweet flavor in tomato sauce can be corrected by adding a small amount of sweated onion and carrot.

_____ 6. Hollandaise sauce should be a lemon-yellow color with a satiny-smooth texture.

_____ 7. A cuisson is often used as the base reduction for a hollandaise sauce.

_____ 8. Beurre blanc is often served with rich foods, such as braised short ribs.

_____ 9. Sauce Maltaise is a derivative of hollandaise.

_____ 10. Sauce Mornay is a derivative of béchamel.

Multiple Choice
Select the single best answer for each

11. Velouté sauces are frequently based upon
    a. milk.
    b. chicken stock.
    c. brown stock.
    d. butter.

12. An example of a pure starch-thickened sauce is
    a. hollandaise.
    b. espagnole.
    c. demi-glace.
    d. jus lié.

13. Which of the following is a derivative of velouté?
    a. Béarnaise.
    b. Bordelaise.
    c. Bercy.
    d. Bretonne.

14. Which of the following is _not_ a derivative of hollandaise?
    a. Bavaroise.
    b. Choron.
    c. Mousseline.
    d. Beurre blanc.

15. Plum tomatoes, or Romas, are generally preferred for making tomato sauces because
    a. they are available year-round.
    b. they are relatively inexpensive.
    c. they have a high ratio of flesh to skin and seed.
    d. they taste better than other tomatoes.

Fill in the Blank
For each space, insert the most appropriate response

16. A basic formula for 1 gallon of white sauce calls for _____, _____, and _____.

17. Liquids that can be used to make a velouté sauce include _____, _____, _____, and _____.

18. The base of a hollandaise sauce can be either _____ or _____.

19. A standard reduction for a beurre blanc is made from _____ and _____.

20. _____ and _____ are two types of brown sauce produced as part of the roasting or sautéing process.

Matching
Select the single best match for each item

_____ 21. Chevreuil   a. Derivative of brown sauce

_____ 22. Vin blanc   b. Derivative of béchamel

_____ 23. Reduced tomato paste or purée   c. Derivative of velouté

_____ 24. Cardinal   d. Derivative of hollandaise

_____ 25. Stock, water, or tomatoes   e. Fixes sweet tomato sauce

_____ 26. Royal   f. Fixes weak tomato sauce

Essay/Short Answer
Answer each question as fully as possible

27. What are the four purposes of sauces? What are the three guidelines for plating sauces?

_____

_____

_____

_____

_____

_____

28. Describe a good-quality hollandaise sauce.

_____

_____

_____

_____

_____

29. Why and how is cream used in a beurre blanc? What is the problem with adding cream?

_____

_____

_____

30. What is the basic formula for 1 gallon of brown sauce? What are four options for finishing "perfect brown sauce," according to the text?

_____

_____

_____

_____

_____

_____

31. What is the basic formula for tomato sauce? What are the quality characteristics of a finished tomato sauce?

_____

_____

_____

_____

_____

_____

CHAPTER 14

<small>SOUPS</small>

Chapter Overview
A well-prepared soup always makes a memorable first impression. Soups offer a full array of flavoring ingredients and garnishing opportunities. Soups also allow the chef to use trimmings and leftovers creatively, an important profit-making consideration for any foodservice establishment.

Chapter Objectives
After reading and studying this chapter, you will be able to
➢ Understand how to properly cook, finish, garnish, reheat, adjust consistency, and degrease clear and thick soups

➢ Prepare and evaluate the quality of clear soups, including consommés, broths, and hearty broths

➢ Prepare and evaluate the quality of thick soups, including purées, cream soups, chowders, and bisques

➢ Understand general guidelines for working with soups

➢ Serve hot and cold soups in the correct manner

Study Outline
Broth

Key Terms and Concepts

broth	double broth	gentle simmer
stock	water	

Consommé

Key Terms and Concepts

basting	clarification	coagulate
consommé	degrease	double consommé
garnish	impurities	raft

Hearty Broths

Key Terms and Concepts

hearty broth	hearty vegetable soup

Cream Soup

Key Terms and Concepts

béchamel

purée soup

velouté soup

cream soup

straining

liaison

velouté

Chowder

Key Terms and Concepts

chaudière

thickener

chowder

hearty broth

Purée Soups

Key Terms and Concepts

legume

purée soup

render

Bisques

Key Terms and Concepts

bisque

vegetable-based bisque

crustacean

thickener

General Guidelines for Soup

Key Terms and Concepts

consistency

flavor and seasoning

serving

degreasing

garnishing

finishing

reheating

Chapter 14 Exercises

True/False

Indicate whether each of the following statements is True (T) or False (F)

_____ 1. A purée soup is slightly thinner than a cream soup and has a somewhat smoother texture.

_____ 2. Meat and poultry broths have a more pronounced flavor than their stock counterparts because they are based on meat rather than bones.

_____ 3. The most common base liquids for purée soups are water, broth, and stock.

_____ 4. Consommés are typically prepared in rondeaus, which give more room for the raft to expand and trap impurities.

_____ 5. Another name for "broth" is "hearty vegetable soup."

_____ 6. Clarification ingredients should be very cold at the start of cooking time.

_____ 7. The lower the heat used to make a consommé, the better.

_____ 8. A chaudière is a "light" or "small" chowder, based on vegetables.

_____ 9. The major distinction between stocks and broths is that broths can be served as is, whereas stocks are used in the production of other dishes.

Multiple Choice
Circle the single best answer for each

10. A cream soup
    a. should have a lightly thickened consistency.
    b. should be thick and chunky.
    c. always includes cream.
    d. is always made with chicken stock.

11. A double broth can be made with _____ as the base liquid.
    a. water.
    b. milk.
    c. remouillage.
    d. wine.

12. Which of the following is *not* typically included in a clarification?
    a. lean ground meat.
    b. onions.
    c. tomatoes.
    d. whole eggs.

13. A vegetable-based bisque is prepared in the same manner as a
    a. purée soup.
    b. chaudière.
    c. cream soup.
    d. hearty vegetable soup.

14. Bisques are traditionally thickened with
    a. roux.
    b. rice.
    c. a liaison.

Fill in the Blank

For each space, insert the most appropriate response

15. In general, the more of a soup's _____ that is exposed to the _____, the _____ the soup will cool.

16. Purée soups are often based on _____ or _____.

17. The raft in a consommé should be _____ to keep it from _____ and potentially _____.

18. The best broths are made from the _____, including meat cuts from the _____ parts of animals.

19. Classically, a cream soup is based on a _____ sauce and finished with _____.

Matching

Select the single best match for each item

_____ 20. Broth

a. Perfectly clear; completely fat-free; rich flavor; discernible body; aromatic

_____ 21. Consommé

b. Rich flavor; velvety texture; lightly thickened consistency

_____ 22. Hearty broth

c. Rich flavor; velvety texture; lightly thickened consistency; classically made from seafood

_____ 23. Cream soup

d. Clear, golden; rich taste; aromatic; good flavor; noticeable body; surface fat

_____ 24. Chowder

e. Slightly coarse or grainy; consistency similar to heavy cream

_____ 25. Bisque

f. Rich color, flavor, and aroma; vegetables give it texture and body

Essay/Short Answer

Answer each question as fully as possible

26. What is a clarification, and why is it used? What are the typical ingredients?

_____

_____

_____

_____

_____

27. What size and consistency should soup garnishes be? What are the three ways of bringing garnishes to service temperature before adding them to soups?

_____

_____

_____

_____

_____

_____

28. What is the basic formula for 1 gallon of meat or poultry broth? For one gallon of fish or shellfish broth? For vegetable broth?

_____

_____

_____

_____

_____

29. Define what is classically meant by "cream soup" and "velouté soup." What is the more contemporary understanding of "cream soup"?

_____

_____

_____

_____

_____

_____

30. Why should cream and liaison soups be finished just prior to service? How should the cream and liaison be added?

_____

_____

_____

_____

_____

_____

CHAPTER **15**

MISE EN PLACE FOR MEATS, POULTRY, AND FISH

Chapter Overview

Bringing out the best flavor in meats, poultry, and fish is a skill that seems to come naturally to a professional chef. Another hallmark of the professional chef is the ability to cook meats, poultry, and fish to the perfect degree of doneness. But in fact these skills are the result of hard work and training: they develop through concentration, practice, and a basic understanding of seasoning and cooking techniques.

Chapter Objectives

After reading and studying this chapter, you will be able to

➢ Understand how and when salt, pepper, and other seasoning ingredients are applied to foods to achieve the desired purposes

➢ Explain how spice blends, dry rubs, and wet marinades are composed and used

➢ Discuss the role of stuffings and describe various types of stuffing

➢ Describe and use the standard breading procedure appropriately and safely

➢ Describe the tests for doneness and how each is applied

➢ List the degree of doneness and final resting temperature for a range of items

Study Outline
Seasonings

Key Terms and Concepts

acid	aromatic	dipping sauce
dry marinade	dry rub	liquid marinade
marinade	marinating times	oil
pepper	salt	seasoning
spice blend	toast	

Stuffings

Key Terms and Concepts

bread stuffing	forcemeat stuffing	grain-based stuffing
stuffing	stuffing and food safety	

Standard Breading

Key Terms and Concepts

breading

chapelure

mie de pain

breading and food safety

crust

standard breading procedure

cross contamination

egg wash

General Guidelines for Determining Doneness in Meats, Poultry, and Fish

Key Terms and Concepts

à la minute

color

final resting temperature

resting

aroma

degree of doneness

internal temperature

tests for doneness

carryover cooking

doneness

resistance

Chapter 15 Exercises

True/False

Indicate whether each of the following statements is True (T) or False (F)

_____ 1. Fresh pork cooked medium will have a final resting temperature of 145°F and will be light pink in color throughout.

_____ 2. Whole turkeys and chickens are rarely stuffed in professional kitchens, as the meat would be overcooked before the stuffing reaches the appropriate temperature.

_____ 3. Another name for a dry rub is "dry marinade."

_____ 4. A good way to control the amount of salt added to a dish is to measure out the amount required by the recipe in advance, so it can be added all at once.

_____ 5. *Chapelure* refers to fresh white bread crumbs, used in the standard breading procedure.

_____ 6. Heat is retained by foods even after they are removed from the heat source.

_____ 7. High-acid marinades are best left in contact with foods for several hours or even overnight.

_____ 8. For food-safety reasons, stuffing in a chicken leg must reach 165°F.

_____ 9. Any unused flour that remains after the standard breading procedure has been completed should be saved for other uses.

_____ 10. The final resting temperature for fish is 145°F, when it is still moist but separates easily into segments.

Multiple Choice

Circle the single best answer for each

11. Seeds and spices are toasted before using to
    a. remove any staleness, making them more crisp.
    b. make them easier to grind.
    c. intensify their flavors.
    d. reduce the likelihood of cross-contamination.

12. All stuffing ingredients that require precooking should be brought to _____ before they are combined with other stuffing ingredients.
    a. 32°F/0°C.
    b. 40°F/4°C.
    c. 135°F/58°C.
    d. 165°F/73°C.

13. Carryover cooking refers to
    a. the amount of extra time it takes stuffing to cook.
    b. the amount of time food continues to cook after being removed from the heat source.
    c. the degree to which the food must be cooked before removal from the heat source.
    d. the "cooking" performed by an acidic marinade to firm or stiffen foods.

14. Marinating times vary according to
    a. whether the item being marinated is a vegetable, grain, or protein.
    b. the texture of the food.
    c. the cooking time.
    d. whether the item will be breaded.

15. Whole birds should have a final resting temperature of
    a. 160°F/70°C.
    b. 170°F/75°C.
    c. 145°F/63°C.
    d. 180°F/82°C.

Fill in the Blank

For each space, insert the most appropriate response

16. _____, including wine and vinegar, are used in marinades to change the _____ and _____ of foods.

17. _____ is the French term for fresh bread crumbs. Dry bread crumbs are called

    _____.

18. Ground chicken or turkey should be cooked to _____. Ground beef should be cooked to _____.

19. Marinades generally contain one or more of the following: _____, _____, and
_____.

20. The _____ is the most efficient way to coat a number of items, using a
consistent sequence; it is a three-step process involving _____, _____, and
_____.

Matching
Select the single best match for each item

_____ 21.	Final resting temperature for rare beef	a. 165°F/74°C
_____ 22.	Final resting temperature for fresh ham	b. 170°F/77°C
_____ 23.	Final resting temperature for poultry breasts	c. 135°F/57°C
_____ 24.	Final resting temperature for medium-rare lamb	d. 145°F/63°C
_____ 25.	Final resting temperature for whole birds	e. 180°F/82°C
_____ 26.	Final resting temperature for stuffing	f. 160°F/71°C

Essay/Short Answer
Answer each question as fully as possible

27. Why is breading performed, and how is it prepared? Define and describe the standard breading
procedure.

_____
_____
_____
_____
_____
_____

28. Why are spices and seeds toasted? Describe two methods of toasting these items.

_____
_____
_____
_____
_____

29. How is a liquid marinade used?

_____
_____
_____

30. Describe the degrees of doneness in the following items: shrimp, scallops, and clams.

_____

_____

_____

_____

_____

_____

31. What senses must a chef rely upon when determining doneness in à la minute cooking? List three and explain.

_____

_____

_____

_____

_____

_____

CHAPTER 16

<small>FABRICATING MEATS, POULTRY, AND FISH</small>

Chapter Overview
Meats, poultry, and fish are among the most costly foods purchased in any kitchen. In this chapter, techniques and methods for trimming, tying, and trussing large cuts or whole birds are explained and illustrated, as are techniques associated with a variety of menu cuts and special cuts known as variety meats. Fish and shellfish fabrication techniques include filleting, preparing paupiettes, shucking, peeling and deveining.

Chapter Objectives
After reading and studying this chapter, you will be able to
➢ Trim fat and silverskin from meats and explain the reasons for doing so

➢ Cut meats into even portions and shape them so that they will cook evenly

➢ Cut portion-size steaks and chops from larger cuts as bone-in and boneless cuts

➢ Prepare certain variety meats

➢ Tie a roast

➢ Grind meats properly for quality and safety

➢ Fabricate poultry suprêmes and côtelettes

➢ Truss poultry for roasting or poaching

➢ Cut chicken into halves and quarters

➢ Disjoint a rabbit

➢ Scale, trim, and gut flat and round fish

➢ Fillet round fish and flat fish

➢ Handle raw and cooked crustaceans

➢ Clean and shuck oysters, clams, and mussels

➢ Clean octopus and squid

Study Outline
Meat Fabrication

Key Terms and Concepts

backbone	bone-in	boneless
chain	châteaubriand	chine bone
chop	cutlet	émincé

escalope
feather bone
grain
grinding
leg
loin
medallion
noisette
portion size
quality
roast
scaloppine
strip loin
tender
tough
tying

fabrication
fell
grenadin
gristle
lip
marrow
membrane
organ meat
pounding
rack
round
silverskin
sweetbreads
tenderloin
tournedos
variety meat

fat
frenching
grinder
kidney
liver
marrow bone
muscle seam
paillard
prefabricated cuts
rib
scallop
steak
tail
tongue
trim
vein steak

Poultry Fabrication

Key Terms and Concepts

backbone
disjoint
foreleg/shoulder
halving
leg
rabbit
suprême
trussing
web skin
wing tip

breast
drumette
free-range
hind legs
oyster
rib cage
tail
trussing needle
wing bone

côtelette
drumstick
frenching
keel bone
quartering
saddle
thigh
tying
wing flap

Fish Fabrication

Key Terms and Concepts

backbone
darne
fillet
fish scaler
gill plate
gutting
pan-dressed
pin bone
round fish
steak
tranche

belly bones
Dover sole
filleting
flat fish
goujonette
hard-boned
paupiette
quarter fillet
scaling skin
straight cut method
up and over method

belly cavity
enzymes
fin
full fillet
grain
head
pectoral fin
roe sack
soft-boned
tail
viscera

Shellfish Fabrication

Key Terms and Concepts

apron	beak	beard
bivalve	butterfly	cephalopod
clam	clam knife	claw meat
coral	crab	crayfish
crustacean	devein	eye
gill filament	half-shell	hinge
ink sac	knuckle	liquor
lobster	mantle	mollusk
mussel	octopus	oyster
oyster knife	peel	quill
shell	shrimp	shuck
skin	soft-shelled crab	squid
suction cups	tail flap	tail portion
tentacles	tomalley	univalve
vein	viscera	wire mesh glove

Chapter 16 Exercises

True/False

Indicate whether each of the following statements is True (T) or False (F)

____ 1. Émincé means "cut into slivers."

____ 2. The technique for a tying a roast with the bone in is very different from that used for a boneless roast.

____ 3. Marrow bones should be soaked in cold, salted water to remove any impurities.

____ 4. Paillards are always pan-fried or sautéed.

____ 5. A scallop is a thin, boneless cut from the loin, tenderloin, or any other sufficiently tender cut of meat.

____ 6. The keel bone is often left attached to the breast when preparing a suprême.

____ 7. The best way to cut a tranche of salmon is to hold the knife so that it will make vertical cuts.

____ 8. A mussel's beard is an indication of the mussel's age.

____ 9. There is a green bubble with an unpleasant flavor in a soft-shelled crab that must be removed before cooking.

____ 10. The straight cut method is typically used to fabricate hard-boned round fish.

Multiple Choice

Circle the single best answer for each

11. The viscera should be removed from a fish as soon as possible because
    a. they are inedible.
    b. the enzymes in the viscera can begin to break down the flesh rapidly, leading to spoilage.
    c. they are poisonous to man.
    d. the smell of the viscera could permeate the flesh.

12. The professional way to remove the pin bones from a salmon and similar fish is to
    a. run a fingertip over the fillet to locate the bones and then pull them out with needlenose pliers.
    b. use a magnifying glass and pliers.
    c. make a V-shaped notch cut down the length of the fish to remove the bones.
    d. make a shallow cut along the side of the fillet to shave away the bones.

13. A paupiette is a
    a. finger-sized fillet, breaded, usually pan-fried.
    b. rolled thin fillet, sometimes stuffed.
    c. pounded cutlet.
    d. steak cut from a round fish, usually broiled or grilled.

14. Châteaubriand is
    a. cut from the thinner end of the tenderloin and typically weighs 5 ounces.
    b. a frenched roast, usually weighing about 2 pounds.
    c. cut from the center of the tenderloin and typically weighs 10 ounces.
    d. a tenderloin which is wrapped in cheesecloth and pounded thin.

15. A leg of veal or lamb can be boned out by
    a. making several parallel cuts down to the bone and peeling away the meat.
    b. pulling out the bone with pliers.
    c. using a band saw to make several cross cuts and then cutting out the pieces of bone from each cut.
    d. using the tip of a boning knife to cut along the natural seams in the meat until the bone is exposed and can be cut away from the meat.

Fill in the Blank

For each space, insert the most appropriate response

16. Whole birds are commonly _____ to give them smooth, compact shapes so they will _____ and _____.

17. The French term for meat that is cut into thin strips or slivers is _____; meat prepared with this technique is generally _____.

18. A medallion or other boneless cut from the loin or tenderloin may be wrapped in cheesecloth and gently shaped, in order to _____ and _____.

19. A semi-boneless poultry breast half with one wing joint left attached is known as a

_____; if skinned, it may be referred to as a _____.

20. Shrimp boiled or steamed in the shell are _____ and _____ than those peeled before cooking.

Matching

Select the single best match for each item

_____ 21. Fell   a. Backbone

_____ 22. Chain   b. Breastbone

_____ 23. Tail   c. Long side muscle on a beef tenderloin

_____ 24. Chine bone   d. Membrane covering a leg of lamb

_____ 25. Aitch bone   e. Pelvic bone

_____ 26. Keel bone   f. Lip on a beef strip loin

Essay/Short Answer

Answer each question as fully as possible

27. Two increasingly popular variety meats are sweetbreads and marrow. How should these items be prepared before cooking?

_____

_____

_____

_____

_____

_____

28. Why are some birds easier than others to fabricate?

_____

_____

_____

_____

_____

29. What is the basic technique for cleaning an octopus? A squid?

_____

_____

_____

_____

_____

30. What is the basic technique for disjointing a rabbit?

_____
_____
_____
_____
_____
_____

31. What is the basic technique for making full fillets of flat fish?

_____
_____
_____
_____
_____
_____

CHAPTER 17

GRILLING AND BROILING, ROASTING AND BAKING

Chapter Overview
Some cooking methods rely on dry heat without fats or oils. The food is cooked either by a direct application of radiant heat (grilling and broiling) or by indirect heat in an oven (roasting and baking). The result of these cooking methods is a highly flavored exterior and a moist interior. Grilling and broiling are quick techniques that are used for naturally tender, portion-size or smaller pieces of meat, poultry, or fish. By contrast, roasting and baking require a longer cooking time and are frequently used with larger cuts of meat, whole birds, and dressed fish.

Chapter Objectives
After reading and studying this chapter, you will be able to
➢ Select and prepare equipment for grilling, broiling, roasting, and baking

➢ Explain what is meant by a "zone" on a grill or broiler and how it can be used to adapt to different foods or different production needs

➢ Clean, preheat, and lubricate a grill or broiler

➢ Grill or broil meats, poultry, and fish to the correct doneness to develop the best flavor and texture in the finished dish

➢ Describe roasting, baking (as it relates to meat, poultry, and fish), smoke roasting, rotisserie cooking, and spit-roasting

➢ Roast or bake meats, poultry, and fish to the correct doneness to develop the best flavor and texture in the finished dish

➢ Describe the correct procedure for preparing a pan gravy and jus

➢ Carve roasts into portions

Study Outline
Grilling and Broiling

Key Terms and Concepts

broil	charred	grill
marked	pan grilling	portion-sized
presentation side	rods	smoky
tender	zone	

Roasting

Key Terms and Concepts

baking	barding	basting
carryover cooking	carving	dripping
instant-read thermometer	jus	larding
pan gravy	pan roasting	rack
resting	roasting	roasting pan
rotisserie cooking	searing	smoke roasting
spit roasting	tender	trussing

Chapter 17 Exercises

True/False

Indicate whether each of the following statements is True (T) or False (F)

_____ 1. Roasted meats should be allowed to rest before they are carved.

_____ 2. Grilled foods must always be prepared à la minute.

_____ 3. An instant-read thermometer is periodically used to calibrate the temperature of an oven.

_____ 4. Jus lié is the French term for pan gravy.

_____ 5. Grill rods should be brushed and rubbed with vegetable oil before preheating.

_____ 6. Although not essential, searing an item before roasting it helps to develop additional flavor and color.

_____ 7. Larding is the technique of tying thin sheets of fat around a food.

_____ 8. A beef rib roast is a large cut which is easiest to handle when turned on its side.

_____ 9. The carving method for a leg of lamb is similar to that used for a ham.

_____ 10. Small roasted items should rest 10 to 15 minutes, medium items for 25 to 30 minutes, and large items for about 1 hour.

Multiple Choice

Circle the single best answer for each

11. Barding is the technique of
    a. soaking meat in a flavorful marinade before roasting.
    b. spitting meat to be roasted.
    c. covering meat with thin sheets of fat before roasting.
    d. inserting small strips of fat back into meat before roasting.

12. The direct application of radiant heat is exemplified by the techniques of
    a. roasting and baking.
    b. grilling and broiling.
    c. roasting and grilling.
    d. roasting and broiling.

13. _____ involves cooking foods on the stove over intense heat in a heavy metal pan with a ridged bottom.
    a. rotisserie cooking.
    b. pan roasting.
    c. smoke roasting.
    d. pan grilling.

14. For banquets, grilled foods can be prepared in advance by
    a. quickly marking the item and then finishing in an oven before service.
    b. grilling the item and then reheating on the grill at service time.
    c. having several chefs grill the item à la minute.
    d. grilling the item and reheating in an oven at service time.

15. Zones on a grill are established to
    a. avoid cross contamination.
    b. extend the life of the grill.
    c. allow more than one grill cook to work together.
    d. avoid flavor transfer.

Fill in the Blank

For each space, insert the most appropriate response

16. A good roasting pan has a _____ with relatively _____ to encourage hot air to circulate freely around the roasting food.

17. The most frequently prepared pan sauces are _____ and _____.

18. _____ on a grill are designated to establish hotter and cooler areas and to avoid _____.

19. _____ lets the temperature of roasted foods equalize, which benefits _____, _____, and _____.

20. Items which are commonly roasted are _____, _____, and _____.

Matching

Select the single best match for each item

_____ 21. Grilling
_____ 22. Broiling
_____ 23. Pan grilling
_____ 24. Roasting
_____ 25. Rotisserie cooking
_____ 26. Smoke roasting

a. Indirect heat surrounds food
b. Food cooks in tightly enclosed environment
c. Radiant heat under food; heavy pan, ridged bottom
d. Radiant heat; food turns on a spit or rod
e. Radiant heat underneath food
f. Radiant heat above food

Essay/Short Answer

Answer each question as fully as possible

27. Explain when and how barbecue sauces should best be applied to foods being grilled.

_____
_____
_____
_____
_____
_____

28. Describe the characteristics of properly prepared grilled or broiled foods.

_____
_____
_____
_____
_____
_____

29. Why is basting used in the roasting process? What is the traditional basting liquid, and what are some alternatives?

_____
_____
_____
_____
_____
_____

30. Describe the characteristics of properly prepared roasted foods. What is the role of color?

_____

_____

_____

_____

_____

_____

31. What is the basic technique for carving ham in the dining room?

_____

_____

_____

_____

_____

_____

CHAPTER **18**

Chapter Overview
The cooking techniques presented in this chapter rely on a fat or oil as the cooking medium. As the amount of fat varies, different effects are achieved.

Chapter Objectives
After reading and studying this chapter, you will be able to
➢ Select and prepare appropriate meats, poultry, or fish for sautéing, pan frying, and deep frying

➢ Sauté, pan fry, and deep fry a variety of foods using the basic methods outlined in the text

➢ Select and prepare appropriate sauces for sautéed foods directly in the sauté pan

➢ Use a safe technique for pan frying

➢ Describe the swimming and basket method for deep frying

➢ Determine doneness and evaluate quality in sautéed, pan-fried, and deep-fried foods

Study Outline
Sautéing

Key Terms and Concepts

au sec	conditioning the pan	deglaze
drippings	dusting	fond
"good color"	monté au beurre	naturally tender
pan sauce	presentation side	sauté
sauté pan	sear	stir fry

Pan Frying

Key Terms and Concepts

breaded	crust	dredged
naturally tender	pan fry	standard breading procedure

Deep Frying

Key Terms and Concepts

basket method	batter	breading
coating	croquette	double-basket method
flavor transfer	naturally tender	recovery time
standard breading procedure	swimming method	

Chapter 18 Exercises

True/False

Indicate whether each of the following statements is True (T) or False (F)

_____ 1. Tempura and other battered deep-fried foods should be dark gold in color.

_____ 2. Breaded items should be prepared à la minute; the crispy coating will quickly deteriorate if stored.

_____ 3. The most appropriate items for sautéing are naturally tender.

_____ 4. Pan-fried items may be finished in the oven to complete cooking.

_____ 5. Pan sauces are usually made to accompany both sautéed and pan-fried items.

_____ 6. The difference between searing and sautéing lies in how the technique is performed.

_____ 7. Pan-frying usually requires more oil than stir-frying and less oil than deep-frying.

_____ 8. Fryer oil should be changed regularly, as old oils have a darker color, more pronounced aroma, and a lower smoke point than fresh oils.

_____ 9. The swimming method is most appropriate for breaded items.

_____ 10. Heating the pan before adding oil is referred to as conditioning the pan.

Multiple Choice

Circle the single best answer for each

11. Foods that would otherwise rise to the surface of the oil too rapidly are deep-fried using the
    a. basket method.
    b. swimming method.
    c. double-basket method.
    d. blanching method, followed by the basket method.

104

12. Heating the sauté pan before adding oil is known as
    a. pre-heating.
    b. searing.
    c. blanching.
    d. conditioning.

13. Stir frying most resembles which cooking technique?
    a. Deep frying.
    b. Sautéing.
    c. Tempura.
    d. Pan frying.

14. Which visual clue indicates that the oil is hot enough to pan fry foods successfully?
    a. There will be a faint haze or slight shimmer on the oil's surface.
    b. The oil just begins to smoke.
    c. Water sizzles and spits when dropped in the pan.
    d. When a corner of the food to be fried is dipped into the oil, its coating will begin to brown within 20 seconds.

15. The primary difference between pan frying and deep frying is
    a. the calorie content of the finished dish.
    b. the amount of fat used to cook the item.
    c. the amount of breading applied to the item.
    d. that pan-fried foods can be held hot longer than deep-fried foods with no loss of quality.

Fill in the Blanks
For each space, insert the most appropriate response

16. The object of sautéing is to produce a _____, resulting from _____.

17. Pan-fried foods are cooked in enough oil to come_____or _____ up their sides and are often cooked over _____ heat than sautéed foods.

18. The three elements which determine color in a pan-fried food are _____, _____, and _____.

19. _____is often applied to the outside of foods to be sautéed to help absorb _____.

20. The optimum temperature for the oil when pan frying is_____; the optimum temperature range for the oil when deep frying is_____.

Matching

Select the single best match for each item

        21. Searing   a. Does not cook food thoroughly

        22. Sautéing   b. Battered food

        23. Stir frying   c. Cooks food in a little fat over high heat

        24. Swimming   d. Cooks small pieces of food in a little fat over high heat

        25. Basket   e. Technique used in sautéing

        26. Conditioning   f. Breaded food

Essay/Short Answer

Answer each question as fully as possible

27. What is recovery time, and why is it important for a chef to understand it?

_____

_____

_____

_____

_____

_____

28. Why should sautéeing foods not be turned too frequently? How often should they be turned and why?

_____

_____

_____

_____

_____

29. What is the swimming method? What is the basket method? Describe both.

_____

_____

_____

_____

_____

30. Describe well-prepared deep-fried food. Why do deep-fried foods become soggy?

_____

_____

_____

_____

_____

31. What fats are appropriate for pan frying? How much fat should be used to cook the food?

_____

_____

_____

_____

_____

CHAPTER 19

STEAMING AND SUBMERSION COOKING

Chapter Overview

Moist-heat techniques – steaming, cooking foods en papillote, shallow poaching, deep poaching, and simmering – rely on liquid and/or water vapor as the cooking medium. Monitoring cooking temperatures and times vigilantly and determining doneness accurately are fundamental to mastering moist-heat methods.

Chapter Objectives

After reading and studying this chapter, you will be able to

➢ Name and describe each of the following moist-heat techniques – steaming, cooking foods en papillote, shallow poaching, deep poaching, and simmering

➢ Select and prepare meats, fish, or poultry for each method discussed

➢ Properly regulate cooking temperatures and determine doneness accurately for each method

➢ Use a variety of techniques to add flavor to foods prepared by these methods

➢ Evaluate the quality of foods prepared by these methods

Study Outline

Steaming

Key Terms and Concepts

albumin	browning	convection steamer
insert	pressure steamer	steaming
tiered steamer	water vapor	

Cooking en Papillote

Key Terms and Concepts

deflate	en papillote	packet
parchment paper	wrapper	

Shallow Poaching

Key Terms and Concepts

aromatics	beurre blanc	cartouche
cuisson	paupiette	sauce vin blanc
shallow poach		

Deep Poaching and Simmering

Key Terms and Concepts

deep poach	instant-read thermometer	shivering
simmer	submerge	

Sous Vide

Key Terms and Concepts

sous vide	protein-tenderizing enzymes	organoleptic qualitities
green merits	hydrolysis	

Chapter 19 Exercises

True/False

Indicate whether each of the following statements is True (T) or False (F)

_____ 1. The pan should be covered during the shallow poaching process.

_____ 2. Foods which are shallow poached should be prepared à la minute.

_____ 3. Deep poached foods are often served with a sauce that is prepared separately.

_____ 4. A food to be cooked sous vide should be at room temperature when placing it into the laminated and extruded plastic bag.

_____ 5. Foods which are shallow poached are cooked with a combination of steam and simmering liquid.

_____ 6. When aromatics are used in shallow poaching, they should be added prior to the main item.

_____ 7. When executed properly, sous vide cooking yields a microbiologically safe product with extended shelf life.

_____ 8. Acids should not be used in the cooking medium when shallow poaching because they will cause the main item to become unpleasantly tough.

_____ 9. The most common preparation for paupiettes is en papillote.

_____ 10. When deep poaching, the surface of the cooking liquid should have small bubbles gently breaking the surface but should not boil rapidly.

Multiple Choice

Circle the single best answer for each

11. When shallow-poaching fish, the presence of white albumin on the surface indicates that the fish
    a. is not fresh.
    b. has been cooked too quickly.
    c. is undercooked.
    d. is just done and should be removed.

12. When shallow poaching, aromatics are generally
    a. sweated or parcooked before the main item is added.
    c. cooked separately and added at the end of the cooking time.
    d. cooked in the cuisson once the main item is removed.
    e. added to the sauce before service.

13. To establish a reliable cooking time for en papillote items, you should
    a. lightly press the main item through the paper with your finger.
    b. use an instant reading thermometer.
    c. perform a few test runs.
    d. allow the package to puff slightly and then deflate.

14. What is the difference in the types of foods used in deep poaching and simmering?
    a. Foods for deep poaching are portion size; foods to be simmered are larger cuts or whole birds.
    b. Foods for deep poaching are tender; foods for simmering are more mature, less tender.
    c. Deep poaching is suitable for poultry and fish; simmering is more suitable for meat.
    d. Foods that are stuffed and tied are always poached; foods that are to be simmered should be left in their natural state.

15. Which of the following is a benefit of sous vide cooking?
    a. a juicier product.
    b. increased yield.
    c. enhanced flavor and nutrition.
    d. all of the above

Fill in the Blank

For each space, insert the most appropriate response

16. With the exception of _____, all moist-heat methods of cooking require the use of _____meat, poultry, or fish.

17. A variation of _____, foods prepared _____are enclosed in a wrapper and baked in a moderate oven.

18. When deep poaching, the liquid should be at _____degrees; when simmering, the liquid should be at _____degrees.

19. Steaming is the technique of using _____as the cooking medium for naturally tender foods within a _____.

20. The basic equipment for sous vide cooking includes _____, _____, _____, _____, _____.

Matching
Select the single best match for each item

_____ 21. Water vapor   a. Parchment paper
_____ 22. Albumin   b. Steam
_____ 23. Cartouche   c. Surface motion
_____ 24. Shiver   d. Rolled fillet
_____ 25. Paupiette   e. Protein
_____ 26. Vin blanc   f. Sauce

Essay/Short Answer
Answer each question as fully as possible

27. Describe the characteristics of properly steamed fish, mollusks, crustaceans, and poultry.

_____
_____
_____
_____
_____
_____
_____

28. How are items to be prepared en papillote assembled and cooked?

_____
_____
_____
_____
_____
_____
_____

29. What is the appropriate amount of liquid to use when shallow poaching and why?

_____

_____

_____

_____

_____

30. Explain the distinguishing factors between deep poaching and simmering.

_____

_____

_____

_____

31. Why is it important that foods being deep poached be completely submerged in the cooking liquid? Should they be covered? Why or why not? What precaution could be taken?

_____

_____

_____

_____

32. Explain the process of sous vide cooking.

_____

_____

_____

_____

CHAPTER **20**

Chapter Overview

Braises and stews are often thought of as peasant dishes because they frequently call for less tender (and less expensive) main ingredients than other techniques. These dishes have a hearty, robust flavor and are often considered fall and winter meals; however, by replacing traditional ingredients with poultry, fish, or shellfish, braises and stews can be faster to prepare, lighter in flavor and color, and appropriate for contemporary menus.

Chapter Objectives

After reading and studying this chapter you will be able to:

➤ Name the similarities and differences between braising and stewing

➤ Select and prepare ingredients and equipment for braises and stews

➤ Prepare a braise or a stew using the basic method

➤ Name a variety of thickening options for stews and braises

➤ Finish a stew with a liaison

➤ Properly determine doneness in a variety of stews and braises

➤ Evaluate the quality of stews and braises

Study Outline

Braises

Key Terms and Concepts

braise	brown braise	connective tissue
fork-tender	light-colored braise	sear
simmer	white braise	

Stews

Key Terms and Concepts

bite-size	blanquette	one-dish meal
sear	simmer	skimming
stew	white stew	

Chapter 20 Exercises

True/False

Indicate whether each of the following statements is True (T) or False (F)

_____ 1. The essential components for stews are the same as for braising; however, stews are prepared with more liquid.

_____ 2. Foods to be braised are typically more mature and less tender than foods to be stewed.

_____ 3. Mirepoix may be puréed and returned to the pot to thicken the sauce for a braise.

_____ 4. Portion-size pieces of meat or poultry are typically used to make a stew.

_____ 5. When braising, the main item should be completely covered by the cooking liquid.

_____ 6. Even though carryover cooking is not as important a factor in braising as it is with dry heat cooking methods, the main item should still be allowed to rest before carving.

_____ 7. When stewing, most main items should be completely covered by the cooking liquid.

_____ 8. White stews and braises are so-called because the main item is not browned before the cooking liquid is added.

_____ 9. When braising, the main item should be cooked just to the point of doneness.

_____ 10. Adding heavy cream or a liaison to a stew is a common finishing and enriching step.

Multiple Choice

Circle the single best answer for each

11. Which of the following is *not* commonly used to thicken the braising liquid for a sauce?
    a. Roux.
    b. Puréed mirepoix.
    c. Heavy cream.
    d. Beurre manié.

12. When preparing a stew, it is best to thicken the sauce
    a. just before serving.
    b. after the vegetables have been cooked and before the liquid is added.
    c. after the main item is fully cooked and all the solid ingredients have been removed.
    d. once the stew has been taken off the direct heat and cooled slightly.

13. White stews are so named because
    a. they are always finished with cream or a liaison.
    b. only white or pale aromatic ingredients are added.
    c. they are only made with white meats and poultry.
    d. the main item is not browned before the cooking liquid is added.

14. White braises are so named because
    a. they are always finished with cream or a liaison.
    b. only white or pale aromatic ingredients are added.
    c. the main item is seared but not browned.
    d. they are only made with white meats and poultry.

15. It is important to remove the cover during the final stages of braising to
    a. reduce the cooking liquid and give the main item a glaze.
    b. reduce the cooking liquid and add the roux.
    c. prevent the main item from overcooking.
    d. reduce the cooking temperature and prevent splattering.

Fill in the Blank

For each space, insert the most appropriate response

16. _____ improves the flavor, texture, and color of the finished dish by removing _____ and _____.

17. One of the benefits of a braise is that virtually all the _____ and _____ are retained in the dish.

18. One of the differences in braising and stewing is the size of the main item: braising uses _____ or _____, while stewing uses _____.

19. Braising concentrates the natural flavors of the _____, the _____, and the _____.

20. Hot air forms a _____ on the surface of a braised item, providing a _____ and _____.

Matching

Select the single best match for each item

_____ 21. Seared deep brown, then partially covered with liquid   a. Stew

_____ 22. Seared to stiffen, then simmered   b. White braise

_____ 23. Onions cooked to a deep golden   c. White stew

_____ 24. Leeks cooked tender and translucent   d. Brown braise

_____ 25. Seared deep brown, then entirely covered with liquid   e. Braise

_____ 26. Liquid added directly to uncooked meat   f. Light-colored braise

Essay/Short Answer

Answer each question as fully as possible

27. What meats are traditionally prepared by braising, and how can they be prepared before cooking?

_____

_____

_____

_____

_____

_____

28. Describe a well-made braise. What indicates overcooking or the use of too high heat?

_____

_____

_____

_____

_____

_____

29. Why is the cooking liquid for a stew brought to a simmer separately? How much should be added to the proteins to be cooked?

_____

_____

_____

_____

_____

_____

30. How is the stewing liquid finished into a sauce?

_____

_____

_____

_____

_____

_____

31. Describe a well-made stew. What indicates overcooking?

_____

_____

_____

_____

_____

_____

CHAPTER 21

MISE EN PLACE FOR VEGETABLES AND FRESH HERBS

Chapter Overview

From trimming and peeling to slicing and dicing, many vegetables and herbs need advance preparation before they are ready to serve or to use as an ingredient in a cooked dish. Various knife cuts are used to shape vegetables and herbs. A thorough mastery of knife skills includes the ability to prepare vegetables and herbs properly for cutting, to use a variety of cutting tools, and to make cuts that are uniform and precise.

Chapter Objectives

After reading and studying this chapter, you will be able to:

➢ Explain the importance of proper vegetable cuts

➢ Perform the basic tasks of vegetable preparation using appropriate tools and techniques

➢ Name the standard cuts and their appropriate dimensions

➢ Cut a variety of vegetables into standard and decorative cuts

➢ Master the specific techniques used for specific vegetables and herbs

➢ Work with dried fruits and vegetables

➢ Describe the general guidelines for vegetable and herb mise en place

Study Outline

Cutting Vegetables and Fresh Herbs

Key Terms and Concepts

allumette	batonnet	bias
brunoise	chiffonade	chopping
diagonal cut	diamond	dicing
fermière	fine brunoise	fine julienne
julienne	large dice	lozenge
matchstick	medium dice	mincing
oblique	paring knife	paysanne
peeling	pommes frites	pommes pont neuf
roll cut	rondelle	shredding
small dice	standard vegetable cuts	swivel-bladed peeler
tourné	uniformity	

Decorative Cuts Using Special Techniques or Tools

Key Terms and Concepts

apple peeler
fluting
mandoline
Parisienne scoop
swivel-bladed peeler
waffle cut

box grater
gaufrette
melon baller
ripple cutter
tourné

fanning
Japanese "turner"
paring knife
safety guard
tourner

Preparation Techniques for Specific Vegetables

Key Terms and Concepts

acidulated water
avocadoes
browning
concassé
filleting
husk
"milking"
peeling
roasting
tomatoes

artichokes
bacterial growth
chestnuts
corn
fresh peppers and chiles
leeks
mushrooms
pit
silk
weeping

asparagus
blanching
choke
edible pods
garlic
mashing
onions
radial cuts
sulfurous odors

Working with Dried Vegetables and Fruits

Key Terms and Concepts

concentration
"plumping"
toasting

long-term storage
preservation

perishability
rehydration

General Guidelines for Vegetable and Herb Mise en Place

consistency
speed

logical flow

proper timing

Chapter 21 Exercises

True/False

Indicate whether each of the following statements is True (T) or False (F)

_____ 1. Chiffonade is a cut used primarily for root vegetables.

_____ 2. Medium-diced vegetables are ¼ x ¼ x ¼ inch cubes.

_____ 3. To clean mushrooms, let them soak in a bowl or sink full of water until there is no sign of dirt; drain carefully.

_____ 4. Leeks should be rinsed under running water until all traces of grit or sand are gone.

_____ 5. To dice vegetables, first trim and cut the vegetable as for the julienne cut.

_____ 6. The shape of the tourné cut is made by cutting a cylindrical vegetable, such as a carrot, crosswise into rounds.

_____ 7. Mincing is a very fine cut that is suitable for onions, shallots, and garlic.

_____ 8. A Parisienne scoop is used to remove the pit from an avocado.

_____ 9. Julienne-cut vegetables are ⅛ x ⅛ x 1- to 2-inch sticks.

_____ 10 Whole and sliced tomatoes can be roasted in the oven to intensify their flavors and change their texture.

Multiple Choice

Circle the single best answer for each

11. This cut is used on long, cylindrical vegetables: the vegetable is cut on a diagonal, turned 90 degrees, and cut again on the same diagonal, forming a piece with two angled edges.
    a. Oblique.
    b. Tourné.
    c. Diagonal.
    d. Brunoise.

12. Which of the following is another term for a diamond cut?
    a. Brunoise.
    b. Paysanne.
    c. Fermière.
    d. Lozenge.

13. It is easier to peel peppers if you first prepare them by
    a. heating them in the oven in a covered pan.
    b. microwaving them for one minute.
    c. holding them over a gas flame until charred.
    d. immersing them in boiling water for 30 seconds.

14. Chiffonade is a vegetable cut usually used for

    a. carrots and turnips.
    b. leafy greens and herbs.
    c. tomatoes and other juicy vegetables.
    d. mushrooms.

15. The waffle or gaufrette cut is most efficiently prepared using a

    a. Parisienne scoop.
    b. paring knife.
    c. swivel-bladed peeler.
    d. mandoline.

Fill in the Blank

For each space, insert the most appropriate response

16. Julienne and batonnet are long, rectangular cuts; related cuts are _____, _____, and _____.

17. Vegetable cuts should be uniform in shape and size so that they _____ and _____.

18. All fresh produce should be thoroughly washed to remove _____, _____, and _____ that might otherwise come in contact with cut surfaces.

19. When tomatoes are _____, _____, and _____, the resulting product is known as tomato concassé.

20. Trimmed artichokes should be held in _____ to prevent _____.

Matching

Select the single best match for each item

_____	21. Tourné	a. ⅛ x ⅛ x 1 to 2 inches
_____	22. Lozenge	b. ⅛ to ½ inches thick
_____	23. Julienne	c. ½ x ½ x ⅛ inches
_____	24. Batonnet	d. ¼ x ¼ x 2 to 2½ inches
_____	25. Rondelle	e. ½ x ½ x ½ inches
_____	26. Medium dice	f. 2 inches long, 7 faces

Essay/Short Answer

Answer each question as fully as possible

27. List the dimensions for the following standard vegetable cuts: fine julienne, julienne, batonnet, fine brunoise, brunoise, small dice, medium dice, and large dice.

_____

_____

_____

_____

_____

_____

28. What is a tourné cut? How is it made, and what are the characteristics of a properly tournéed vegetable?

_____

_____

_____

_____

_____

_____

29. What is a fan cut? How is it made, and for what items is it appropriate?

_____

_____

_____

_____

_____

_____

30. How should garlic be mashed? Why is salt often used?

_____

_____

_____

_____

_____

31. What is the purpose of coarse chopping? How is it done? How should the finished product appear?

_____

_____

_____

_____

CHAPTER 22

COOKING VEGETABLES

Chapter Overview

Vegetables are far more important in contemporary menu planning than simply side dishes. They can be the focal part of a meatless entrée. They can be selected and prepared to enhance another dish. Or they can be served as an appetizer or hors d'oeuvre. Buying vegetables that are at the peak of quality, observing proper storage and handling standards, and giving meticulous attention to the cooking process are vital to producing an appealing vegetable dish.

Chapter Objectives

After reading and studying this chapter, you will be able to:

➢ Describe a variety of techniques for cooking vegetables

➢ Evaluate vegetables cooked by various techniques according to the appropriate quality standards

➢ Explain how to prepare vegetables in advance to improve efficiency during service periods

➢ Select and prepare ingredients and equipment for a variety of cooking methods

Study Outline

Boiling

Key Terms and Concepts

acid	al dente	blanch
boil	green vegetables	parboil
parcook	red or white vegetables	refresh
root vegetables	shock	tender-crisp

Steaming

Key Terms and Concepts

convection steamer	insert	pressure steamer
steam	tiered steamer	vapor bath

Pan Steaming

Key Terms and Concepts

condensation	glaze	pan sauce
pan steam	sweetener	

Grilling and Broiling

Key Terms and Concepts

broil	broiler	carry-over cooking
char	cross-hatch	flare-up
grill	hand grill	marinade
parcook	raw	rods
sizzler platter		

Roasting and Baking

Key Terms and Concepts

bake	blender	browning
dry heat	food mill	food processor
hot spots	marinade	purée
ricer	roast	rotate
sieve	vertical chopping machine	

Sautéing

Key Terms and Concepts

finishing	glazing	recovering heat
sauté	stir-fry	wok

Pan Frying

Key Terms and Concepts

batter	breading	overcrowding
pan frying		

Deep Frying

Key Terms and Concepts

basket method	batch	batter
breading	croquette	deep fryer
deep frying	fritter	frying kettle
recovery time	seasoning	swimming method
tempura-style		

Stewing and Braising

Key Concepts and Terms

braise	brasier	fork tender
holding	meltingly soft	rondeau
stew		

General Guidelines for Vegetables

Key Concepts and Terms

advance cooking	appropriate doneness	batch cooking
quality	reheating	tender

Chapter 22 Exercises

True/False

Indicate whether each of the following statements is True (T) or False (F)

_____ 1. All vegetables that will be grilled should first be blanched or parboiled.

_____ 2. To finish vegetables in whole butter or heavy cream, they should be repeatedly tossed over brisk heat until they are very hot and evenly coated.

_____ 3. Denser green vegetables, such as broccoli, should be boiled, covered, to allow the natural acid to retain the vegetable's color.

_____ 4. When reheating vegetables in the microwave, use a low setting on the microwave to reheat them gently and slowly.

_____ 5. The boiling method varies depending on the color of the vegetables to be cooked.

_____ 6. When steaming, the color and type of vegetable will determine whether the pot should be covered.

_____ 7. When pan-steaming vegetables, the cooking liquid may be reduced to make a sauce or form a glaze.

_____ 8. When roasting vegetables, the fond from the vegetables is usually reduced to make a sauce for the dish.

_____ 9. Pan frying requires more fat than sautéing, but less than deep frying.

_____ 10. With the exception of potatoes, most vegetables roast better if they are peeled before baking.

Multiple Choice
Circle the single best answer for each

11. One reason that vegetables are blanched is to
    a. cook them so they can be finished quickly at service time.
    b. reduce any strong odors or flavors.
    c. limit the potential for bacterial growth before cooking.
    d. make them more flavorful and nutritious.

12. Pan steaming is best suited for
    a. small batches of vegetables prepared à la minute.
    b. root vegetables.
    c. large quantities, using a pressure steamer.
    d. vegetables that will be served with the skin or peel intact.

13. In which of the following techniques are the cooked vegetables *not* frequently finished by glazing?
    a. Broiling.
    b. Pan steaming.
    c. Steaming.
    d. Sautéing.

14. The amount of time that fryer oil needs to regain its proper temperature after vegetables have been added to it is known as
    a. blanching.
    b. recovery time.
    c. finishing.
    d. the smoking point.

15. The correct temperature for deep frying vegetables is generally
    a. 325°F/165°C.
    b. 350°F/177°C.
    c. 375°F/190°C.
    d. 400°F/205°C.

Fill in the Blank
For each space, insert the most appropriate response

16. Two techniques for deep-frying vegetables are the _____, used for _____ items, and the _____, used for _____ items.

17. Properly steamed vegetables should have _____ and _____.

18. Grilled vegetables typically have a _____ flavor with _____ exteriors and interiors which are _____ with an _____.

19. Tomatoes and peppers are often roasted to _____ and _____.

126

20. When used to glaze vegetables, sugars liquefy and may be allowed to caramelize, coating the vegetables evenly to give it _____, _____, and _____.

Matching

Select the single best match for each item

_____ 21. Sautéing   a. Small amount of fat; often finished by glazing

_____ 22. Stir-frying   b. Moderate amount of fat; often breaded or battered

_____ 23. Steaming   c. Small amount of fat; served directly from the cooking vessel

_____ 24. Pan steaming   d. Good nutritional value; small quantities of vegetables

_____ 25. Pan frying   e. Large amount of fat; often breaded or battered

_____ 26. Deep frying   f. Good nutritional value; small or large quantities

Essay/Short Answer

Answer each question as fully as possible

27. The equipment used to process puréed foods has a significant effect on the finished product. Describe the results obtained by using food mills, food processors, and blenders.

_____

_____

_____

_____

_____

_____

28. What are the characteristics of properly pan-fried vegetables? List three ways in which this technique differs from sautéing.

_____

_____

_____

_____

_____

_____

29. What are the characteristics of properly deep-fried vegetables?

_____

_____

_____

_____

_____

_____

30. List three ways in which a sauce for braised or stewed vegetables may be prepared from the cooking liquid. What are the characteristics of properly braised or stewed vegetables?

_____

_____

_____

_____

_____

31. How does the boiling process change for different types of vegetables?

_____

_____

_____

_____

_____

CHAPTER 23

COOKING POTATOES

Chapter Overview

The potato is one of the most versatile foods in the world. It is found in nearly every menu category as the main component of appetizers, soups, entrees, and side dishes; it is also an important ingredient in such preparations as soufflés, pancakes, and breads.

Chapter Objectives

After reading and studying this chapter, you will be able to:

➢ Name the three basic categories of potatoes and explain how moisture and starch content affects the characteristics of the potato after cooking

➢ Distinguish potato varieties according to their starch and moisture content and list appropriate preparations made from them

➢ Select and prepare potatoes, other ingredients, and equipment for a variety of cooking methods: boiling, steaming, puréeing, baking en casserole, baking and roasting, sautéing, and deep frying

➢ Name a variety of familiar potato dishes and the cooking methods used to prepare them

➢ Prepare potatoes according to the standard methods

➢ Determine proper doneness in potatoes and evaluate potato dishes for quality according to the appropriate standards

Study Outline

Potato Varieties

Key Terms and Concepts

all-purpose potatoes	baking potatoes	boiling potatoes
chef's potatoes	fingerling potatoes	high moisture/low starch
Idaho potatoes	low moisture/high starch	Maine potatoes
moderate moisture and starch	"new" potatoes	red-skinned potatoes
russet potatoes	starch	US 1 potatoes
waxy yellow potatoes		

Boiling Potatoes

Key Terms and Concepts

boiling	brine	discoloration
draining	drying	en chemise
high-moisture potatoes	low-moisture potatoes	moderate-moisture potatoes
solanine	steaming	

Puréeing Potatoes

Key Terms and Concepts

croquettes	duchesse potatoes	food mill
low-moisture potatoes	moderate-moisture potatoes	overworking
pommes lorette	potato ricer	puréeing

Baking and Roasting Potatoes

Key Terms and Concepts

baking	high-moisture potatoes	low-moisture potatoes
mealy	oven-roasting	soggy
stuffed potatoes	twice-baked potatoes	waxy yellow potatoes

Baking Potatoes En Casserole

Key Terms and Concepts

au gratin potatoes	cream	custard
en casserole	dauphinoise potatoes	gratin
hot-water bath	low-moisture potatoes	mandoline
scalloped potatoes	waxy yellow potatoes	

Sautéing Potatoes

Key Terms and Concepts

crust	hash browns	home fries
Lyonnaise potatoes	moderate-moisture potatoes	potatoes Anna
potato pancakes	rösti	sautéing

Deep Frying Potatoes

Key Terms and Concepts

allumette potatoes	blanching	deep frying
French fries	gaufrette potatoes	low-moisture potatoes
matchstick potatoes	shoestring potatoes	soufflé potatoes
steak fries	waffle-cut potatoes	

Chapter 23 Exercises

True/False

Indicate whether each of the following statements is True (T) or False (F)

_____ 1. Before deep frying potatoes, parboil them first to ensure that they will have the proper color, texture, and flavor.

_____ 2. High-moisture potatoes are best for baking, since there is less likelihood of their becoming mealy.

_____ 3. Moderate moisture and starch potatoes are frequently used in salads and soups because they maintain their shape during cooking.

_____ 4. Peeled potatoes should be submerged in water to eliminate the toxin solanine; the water should be changed regularly to leach out as much solanine as possible.

_____ 5. En chemise refers to potatoes that will be boiled in their skins.

_____ 6. The liquid most commonly used for making puréed potatoes is hot water.

_____ 7. Eggs or pâte à choux are sometimes blended with potato purée before deep frying.

_____ 8. Many en casserole dishes are referred to as gratins.

_____ 9. Blenders or food processors should never be used when puréeing potatoes, since the texture of the potato may become soupy, sticky, and unable to hold its shape.

_____ 10. Moderate-moisture potatoes give the best texture and appearance to sautéed dishes.

Multiple Choice

Circle the single best answer for each

11. _____ are appropriate for en casserole dishes.
    a. Low-moisture potatoes.
    b. Moderate-moisture potatoes.
    c. High-moisture potatoes.
    d. All parcooked potatoes.

12. _____ are appropriate for deep-fried dishes.
    a. Low-moisture potatoes.
    b. Moderate-moisture potatoes.
    c. High-moisture potatoes.
    d. All parcooked potatoes.

13. _____ are appropriate for puréed dishes.
   a. Fingerling potatoes.
   b. "New" potatoes.
   c. Russet and waxy yellow potatoes.
   d. Any properly cooked potatoes.

14. All-purpose and chef's potatoes fall into the _____ category.
   a. low moisture/high starch.
   b. moderate moisture/high starch.
   c. moderate moisture and starch.
   d. high moisture/low starch.

15. Idaho and russet potatoes fall into the _____ category.
   a. low moisture/high starch.
   b. moderate moisture/high starch.
   c. moderate moisture and starch.
   d. high moisture/low starch.

Fill in the Blanks

For each space, insert the most appropriate response

16. It takes approximately _____for a 6-ounce/170-gram potato to bake. Once baked, it should be _____ or _____.

17. Sautéed potatoes combine a _____ exterior with a _____ interior and are predominantly flavored by the _____ used.

18. The naturally sweet, fresh flavor of "new" potatoes is best showcased by simple techniques, such as _____, _____, and _____.

19. Raw potatoes _____ after peeling, turning first _____ and eventually _____; prevent this by _____.

Matching

Select the single best match for each item

_____ 20. Solanine	a. Unpeeled	
_____ 21. En chemise	b. Characteristic of sautéed potatoes	
_____ 22. En casserole	c. Moist and tender, with a thick and smooth sauce	
_____ 23. Gratin	d. Associated with deep frying	
_____ 24. Blanch	e. Toxin found in potato sprouts and eyes	
_____ 25. Crust	f. Type of en casserole preparation	

Essay/Short Answer

Answer each question as fully as possible

26. Describe low moisture/high starch potatoes. How are they used? What potatoes fall into this category?

_____

_____

_____

_____

_____

_____

27. Describe moderate moisture and starch potatoes. How are they used? What potatoes fall into this category?

_____

_____

_____

_____

_____

_____

28. Describe high moisture/low starch potatoes. How are they used? What potatoes fall into this category?

_____

_____

_____

_____

_____

29. What is the process for deep frying potatoes?

_____

_____

_____

_____

_____

30. What is the process for sautéing potatoes?

_____

_____

_____

_____

_____

CHAPTER 24

COOKING GRAINS AND LEGUMES

Chapter Overview

One of the most dramatic changes on the culinary scene in recent years has been the rediscovery of grains and legumes. Everyday grains – wheat, corn, rice – are appearing in many new forms, and beans have become more popular as well. In addition, exotic grains, such as millet and quinoa, and beans that were once rarely seen, including flageolets and borlottis, are appearing more and more frequently.

Chapter Objectives

After reading and studying this chapter, you will be able to:

➢ Select the proper advance preparation method for a variety of grains and legumes

➢ Name the two basic approaches to soaking legumes and discuss reasons why and why not to soak legumes

➢ Select and prepare grains and legumes, other ingredients, and equipment for a variety of cooking methods: boiling (simmering), steaming, pilaf, and risotto

➢ Name a variety of familiar grain and legume dishes and the cooking method used to prepare them

➢ Prepare grains and legumes according to the standard methods

➢ Determine proper doneness in grains and legumes and evaluate dishes for quality according to the appropriate standards

Study Outline

Simmering Whole Grains and Legumes

Key Terms and Concepts

bran	grain	legume
long soak	oligosaccharides	rehydrate
short soak	soak	sort

Simmering and Boiling Cereals and Meals

Key Terms and Concepts

bran	cereal	coarse
fine	flour	germ
meal	milling	processing
whole grain		

Pilaf

Key Terms and Concepts

gelatinization	grain	onion
parching	pilau	pilaf
rice		

Risotto

Key Terms and Concepts

all'onda	Arborio	Carnaroli
medium-grain round rice	risotto	Vialone Nane
wine		

Chapter 24 Exercises

True/False

Indicate whether each of the following statements is True (T) or False (F)

_____ 1. Cereal and grain meals are usually cooked in just as much liquid as they can absorb, but each type will absorb a different amount of liquid.

_____ 2. Legumes should be completely covered by liquid at all times during the cooking process.

_____ 3. Polenta should be stirred as little as possible; stirring may cause starch granules to burst, creating a gluey texture.

_____ 4. Legumes should be cooked just until done; they should retain their shape and still be slightly firm to the bite.

_____ 5. A member of the onion family is usually required for a pilaf.

_____ 6. Heating the grain in hot fat or oil is called parching.

_____ 7. When preparing risotto, the cooking liquid should be brought to a simmer separately.

_____ 8. When preparing pilaf, the cooking liquid should be added cold/room temperature to give additional texture to the grains.

_____ 9. Cheese is added to risotto after the rice has absorbed one-third of the cooking liquid in order to impart a deep, rich flavor without scorching.

_____ 10. The soaking liquid from legumes is generally discarded, as it contains dust and sediments.

Multiple Choice

Circle the single best answer for each

11. Parching refers to the practice of
    a. drying the grains on a sheet tray after they have soaked.
    b. cooking a meal or cereal until it becomes stiff enough to pull away from the sides of the pot.
    c. cooking grains in a small amount of stock until the liquid is absorbed, at which time more liquid is added.
    d. heating grains in hot fat or oil before adding a liquid.

12. _____ is typically soaked in boiling liquid for several minutes.
    a. Bulgur wheat.
    b. Polenta.
    c. Domestic basmati rice.
    d. Pearl barley.

13. One difference between the short soak and long soak methods is that
    a. the short soak method uses hot liquid and the long soak method uses cold liquid.
    b. the short soak method uses more liquid than the long soak method.
    c. the long soak method uses hot liquid and the short soak method uses cold liquid.
    d. the long soak method uses more liquid than the short soak method.

14. Polenta refers to
    a. a preparation of long-grain rice which is heated in a pan and then cooked with hot liquid.
    b. any cereal or meal that is cooked in hot liquid, cooled in a sheet pan, and cut into shapes to be reheated.
    c. an Italian rice dish cooked to a porridge-like consistency.
    d. ground cornmeal added to a simmering liquid and cooked to a smooth creamy consistency.

15. Adding salt to legumes at the beginning of the cooking process
    a. raises the temperature of the liquid, shortening the cooking time.
    b. causes the legumes to be seasoned more thoroughly than if the salt were withheld until the end of cooking.
    c. softens the water, making the beans softer and creamier.
    d. toughens the skins, lengthening the cooking time.

Fill in the Blank

For each space, insert the most appropriate response

16. Culinary grains may go through some type of processing, called _____, before they reach the kitchen to produce _____ and _____.

17. _____ is a Middle Eastern dish in which the _____, typically _____, is _____ and then combined with a hot liquid.

18. If the liquid used to cook legumes is completely _____, the legumes might _____ or _____.

19. When the water used to soak legumes is used as the cooking liquid for the legumes, the _____, _____, and _____ are retained, but so are the _____.

20. _____ is a porridge-like dish made with _____; when properly prepared; it is described as _____, or wavelike.

Matching

Select the single best match for each item

_____ 21. Imported basmati rice
_____ 22. Domestic jasmine rice
_____ 23. Legume
_____ 24. Coarse cereal
_____ 25. Pilaf
_____ 26. Oligosaccharides

a. Not soaked
b. Indigestible sugars
c. Soaked
d. Typically cooked with stock
e. Dense, porridge-like texture
f. Covered by liquid at all times while cooking

Essay/Short Answer

Answer each question as fully as possible

27. Why do some chefs believe legumes should be soaked, but some chefs do not?

_____
_____
_____
_____
_____
_____

28. Describe the process for cooking cereals or meals.

_____

_____

_____

_____

_____

29. What is parching? Why is it performed? Name two techniques for cooking grains in which parching plays a role.

_____

_____

_____

_____

_____

30. What are the characteristics of a properly prepared pilaf? Describe overcooked and undercooked pilafs.

_____

_____

_____

_____

_____

31. What are the three basic points at which flavoring and/or seasoning may be added to a risotto, and what types of flavoring and seasoning agents are added at each point?

_____

_____

_____

_____

_____

CHAPTER **25**

Chapter Overview

The immense popularity of pastas and dumplings is not at all surprising. Nutritious and highly versatile, these foods are an important element of most cuisines. They are based on ingredients that are inexpensive and easy to store: flour, meal, and eggs. They adapt well to a number of uses and can be found on contemporary menus as appetizers, entrées, salads, and even desserts.

Chapter Objectives

After reading and studying this chapter, you will be able to

➢ Identify key similarities and differences between fresh and dried pastas

➢ Select and prepare ingredients and equipment for preparing fresh pasta, noodles, and dumplings

➢ Cook fresh and dried pastas to the correct doneness

➢ Name the correct procedures for preparing pastas in advance

➢ Roll and cut fresh pasta by hand or using a machine

➢ Use the general guidelines on fresh and dried pastas for serving and reheating

Study Outline

Making Fresh Pasta, Noodles, and Dumplings

Key Terms and Concepts

batter	dough	dried pasta
dumpling	eggs	flour
fresh pasta	oil	pasta machine
spätzle		

Cooking Pasta and Noodles

Key Terms and Concepts

al dente	extruded noodles	filled pasta
flat noodles	holding	mushy
sauce	tube pasta	twisted pasta

General Guidelines for Serving Pasta

Key Terms and Concepts

à la carte service   banquet service   buffet service

Chapter 25 Exercises

True/False

Indicate whether each of the following statements is True (T) or False (F)

_____ 1.   Dumplings are a specific type of fresh pasta, always served with stews and ragouts.

_____ 2.   Oil is frequently used in pasta dough to keep the dough pliable and easy to knead.

_____ 3.   Fresh pasta can be mixed using a food processor or electric mixer.

_____ 4.   Spätzle is made by forcing the dough through a pasta extrusion machine.

_____ 5.   In general, noodles can be mixed and prepared in the same manner as fresh pasta.

_____ 6.   Dim sum is the term for Chinese pot stickers.

_____ 7.   Fresh pasta and noodles can be covered and refrigerated for up to 2 days.

_____ 8.   When cooking pasta, the amount of water needed will vary depending on whether the pasta is dry or fresh.

_____ 9.   The Italian term "al dente" literally translates "to the death."

_____ 10   A hearty sauce most successfully complements the delicate flavor of fresh pasta.

Multiple Choice

Circle the single best answer for each

11. When preparing pasta dough in a food processor, the blended dough should appear
    a.   soft and pliable.
    b.   smooth and elastic.
    c.   like a coarse meal.
    d.   firm and stiff.

12. After kneading and resting, the pasta dough should appear
    a.   soft and pliable.
    b.   smooth and elastic.
    c.   like a coarse meal.
    d.   firm and stiff.

13. After kneading, pasta dough must rest/relax
    a. at least 15 minutes.
    b. at least one hour.
    c. overnight in the refrigerator.
    d. overnight at room temperature.

14. The ratio of water to pasta is
    a. 1 pint of water to 1 pound of pasta.
    b. 1 quart of water to 1 pound of pasta.
    c. 1 gallon of water to 1 pound of pasta.
    d. equal parts pasta and water.

15. In general, filled pasta require only a
    a. very light sauce.
    b. meat sauce.
    c. sauce that is at least flavorful as it is filling.
    d. sauce with garnish of fresh vegetables.

Fill in the blank

For each space, insert the most appropriate response

16. The three basic ways to mix pasta dough are _____, _____ or
    _____.

17. Eggs are frequently included in fresh pasta to provide _____,
    _____, and _____.

18. Long, flat pastas are generally served with _____, _____ sauces that will
    _____.

19. _____ can be simmered, poached, or baked; they may also be _____,
    _____, or _____.

20. As pasta cooks, it becomes _____ throughout; an _____ shows that the
    pasta is not completely cooked.

Matching

Select the single best match for each item

_____ 21. Long, flat pasta
_____ 22. Tube or twisted pasta
_____ 23. Fresh pasta
_____ 24. Dried pasta
_____ 25. Banquet service
_____ 26. Buffet service

a. Meat sauces
b. Hotel pans
c. Bowls or deep platters
d. Cooked to order
e. Cream sauces
f. Cooked in advance

Essay/Short Answer

Answer each question as fully as possible

27. Describe proper storage procedures for fresh pasta. How should fresh pasta be stored over long periods of time?

_____
_____
_____
_____
_____
_____

28. What is the proper procedure for mixing pasta dough by hand?

_____
_____
_____
_____
_____

29. How should cooked pasta be reheated for service?

_____
_____
_____
_____
_____

30. What types of sauce are appropriate for fresh pasta? For dried pasta? For filled pasta?

_____

_____

_____

_____

_____

_____

31. How is pasta prepared and served for à la carte service? For banquet service? For buffet service?

_____

_____

_____

_____

_____

_____

CHAPTER 26

COOKING EGGS

Chapter Overview

Eggs can be served at virtually any meal, as part of every course. They can be cooked in the shell, poached, fried, scrambled, or prepared as omelets or soufflés. Using fresh eggs for cooking is important to ensure the best flavor and quality in the finished dish. The top grade of eggs, AA, indicates that the eggs are fresh. They will have a white that does not spread excessively once the egg is cracked, and the yolk should ride high on the white's surface. Proper cooking of eggs is also essential to the quality of the finished dish. Regardless of the recipe or cooking method used, when eggs are overcooked, excessive coagulation of the proteins forces water out and the eggs become dry.

Chapter Objectives

After reading and studying this chapter you will be able to:

➢ Select and prepare eggs (and other ingredients as required) and equipment for specific egg preparations

➢ Cook eggs in the shell to a range of doneness and evaluate the quality of eggs cooked in the shell

➢ Poach eggs properly and hold them for service

➢ Fry eggs to a variety of doneness and evaluate their quality according to the appropriate standards

➢ Scramble eggs properly and name the characteristics of properly scrambled eggs

➢ Identify the different styles of omelets and describe the methods for each style and their quality characteristics

➢ Make a savory soufflé that rises properly and has a light texture

Study Outline

Cooking Eggs in the Shell

Key Terms and Concepts

bare simmer	boil	coagulation
coddled egg	hard-boiled egg	peel
shell	soft-boiled egg	sulfur

Poaching Eggs

Key Terms and Concepts

Eggs Benedict	Eggs Florentine	poached egg
salt	shelled egg	teardrop
underpoach	vinegar	

Frying Eggs

Key Terms and Concepts

American-style	baste	blister
browning	fried egg	huevos rancheros
over	shirred egg	sunny-side up
sur le plat		

Scrambling Eggs

Key Terms and Concepts

blend	coagulate	curd
scrambled egg	texture	water bath
weeping		

Making Omelets

Key Terms and Concepts

American-style	filling	flat omelet
folded omelet	French style	frittata
rolled omelet	souffléed omelet	

Savory Soufflés

Key Terms and Concepts

base	beaten egg whites	béchamel
lightener	savory	soufflé
sweet	timing	

Chapter 26 Exercises

True/False

Indicate whether each of the following statements is True (T) or False (F)

_____ 1. Like sweet soufflés, savory soufflés typically use pastry cream as a base.

_____ 2. The green ring surrounding the yolk in a hard-cooked egg indicates that the egg is not very fresh.

_____ 3. For a large curd with a creamy texture, stir scrambling eggs infrequently.

_____ 4. Boiled eggs in the shell should be cooked in water that is at or close to a simmer.

_____ 5. Poached eggs can be prepared in advance and held safely throughout a service period.

_____ 6. Both flat and folded omelets are baked in an oven.

_____ 7. Adding vinegar and salt to the poaching liquid encourages the protein in eggs to set more quickly.

_____ 8. Although beaten egg whites are critical to the success of a savory soufflé, egg yolks are never used in this dish.

_____ 9. The base mixture for soufflés provides structure that helps keep the soufflé from collapsing after it is removed from the oven.

_____ 10. Raw eggs with cracked shells should be checked for a strong sulfur smell.

Multiple Choice

Circle the single best answer for each

11. Any eggs with cracked shells should be
    a. used for scrambled preparations.
    b. cooked immediately.
    c. discarded immediately.
    d. checked for a strong sulfur smell.

12. Which of the following is *not* an example of an egg cooked in its shell?
    a. deviled.
    b. coddled.
    c. shirred.
    d. soft-cooked.

13. Shelled eggs should be added to the poaching liquid when it reaches
    a. 165°F/73°C.
    b. 180°F/82°C.
    c. 212°F/100°C.
    d. 425°F/220°C.

14. Soufflés should be baked in an oven heated to
    a. 212°F/100°C.
    b. 350°F/175°C.
    c. 375°F/190°C.
    d. 425°F/218°C.

15. The ideal temperature range for frying eggs is
    a. 165° to 175°F/73° to 80°C.
    b. 180° to 212°F/82° to 100°C.
    c. 255° to 280°F/124° to 138°C.
    d. 300° to 325°F/150° to 165°C.

Fill in the Blank

For each space, insert the most appropriate response

16. Three examples of flat omelets are the _____, the _____, and the _____.

17. The _____ the _____ and the _____ the _____, the creamier the finished scrambled eggs will be.

18. Properly fried eggs have _____ whites and a _____; they are not _____ or _____.

19. To make scrambled eggs puffier, add _____ per each beaten egg.

20. The American-style _____ omelet is prepared in a small sauté pan in a manner similar to the French-style _____ omelet.

Matching

Select the single best match for each item

_____ 21. 3-minute egg   a. 255° to 280°F/124° to 138°C
_____ 22. Poached egg   b. Starts in simmering water
_____ 23. Fried egg   c. Beaten whites are folded into beaten yolks
_____ 24. Scrambled egg   d. Beaten whites are folded into a base
_____ 25. Souffléed omelet   e. May be cooked over a water bath
_____ 26. Savory soufflé   f. Starts in simmering, acidulated, seasoned water

Essay/Short Answer

Answer each question as fully as possible

27. Describe the appearance of a properly prepared rolled omelet, folded omelet, flat omelet, and souffléed omelet.

_____

_____

_____

_____

_____

28. What guidelines are effective in preventing the shells of hard-boiled eggs from cracking? What two myths are ineffective?

_____
_____
_____
_____
_____

29. What is the green ring which sometimes surrounds the yolk of a hard-cooked egg? What causes it to form, and how can it be avoided?

_____
_____
_____
_____
_____

30. Why are poached eggs sometimes prepared in advance and held throughout service? How are they held and reheated?

_____
_____
_____
_____
_____

31. What are the characteristics of a properly poached egg?

_____
_____
_____
_____
_____

CHAPTER **27**

Salad Dressings and Salads

Chapter Overview

Salads appear on the menu in so many different guises today that it is easy to imagine that they were invented by this generation of chefs. In fact, fresh concoctions of seasoned herbs and lettuces have been relished in every part of the world from the beginning of recorded culinary history.

Chapter Objectives

After reading and studying this chapter, you will be able to:

➤ Use the basic ratios and methods to prepare vinaigrettes and mayonnaise

➤ Describe how to rescue a broken mayonnaise

➤ Evaluate the quality of salad dressings according to the correct quality standards

➤ Name the purposes for a green salad

➤ Select and combine salad greens and wash, dry, and store them properly

➤ Prepare flavored oils and vinegars and store them properly

➤ Select and prepare a variety of fresh fruits for salads

➤ Select and prepare ingredients and dressings for warm, vegetable, potato, pasta, grain, legume, and composed salads

Study Outline

Vinaigrette

Key Terms and Concepts

acid	balance	emulsifier
flavored oil	flavored vinaigrette	infuse
oil	standard vinaigrette ratio	temporary emulsion
vinaigrette		

Mayonnaise

Key Terms and Concepts

broken mayonnaise
lecithin
salmonella

cold sauce
mayonnaise
stable emulsion

grand sauce
pasteurized egg yolks

Green Salads

Key Terms and Concepts

crouton
green salad
mixed salad

dress
hydroponically
spinner

garden salad
mesclun
tossed salad

Fruit Salads

Key Terms and Concepts

acidulate
"eyes"
oxidize

blanch
hedgehog cut
suprême

brown
mandoline
zest

Warm Salads

Key Terms and Concepts

bed

salade tiède

warm salad

Vegetable Salads

Key Terms and Concepts

composed salad
legume salad
raw vegetable salad

cooked vegetable salad
pasta salad

grain salad
potato salad

Chapter 27 Exercises

True/False

Indicate whether each of the following statements is True (T) or False (F)

_____ 1. To remove the core from heading lettuce, use a paring knife or gently rap the lettuce down on a work surface.

_____ 2. To avoid bruising the lettuce, it should be torn rather than cut into bite-size pieces.

_____ 3. A vinaigrette is an example of a temporary emulsion.

_____ 4. Vinaigrettes should rest for at least one hour before using.

_____ 5. A finished mayonnaise should be thick enough to hold soft peaks.

_____ 6. Citrus suprêmes are made by cutting along each side of the membranes that divide the citrus segments within the peeled fruit.

_____ 7. When preparing mayonnaise by hand, the oil must be added slowly; when preparing mayonnaise by machine, the oil may be added all at once.

_____ 8. Bean salads should not be dressed and allowed to rest for extended periods, as the acid in the dressing will cause the skins of the cooked legumes to toughen.

_____ 9. Dressed pasta and grain salads can be held for up to 2 days without losing quality.

_____ 10. To avoid having croutons become greasy, they should be baked rather than fried.

Multiple Choice

Circle the single best answer for each

11. The best way for chefs to avoid foodborne illnesses when preparing mayonnaise is to
    a. heat the yolks over a bain marie, without cooking them.
    b. use only egg whites in the preparation.
    c. hold the mayonnaise at the proper temperature (under refrigeration).
    d. use pasteurized egg yolks.

12. Aïoli is
    a. a flavored, garnished mayonnaise most often served with fish.
    b. a type of mayonnaise prepared with a mortar and pestle.
    c. a garlic mayonnaise.
    d. a cold sauce prepared with garlic, basil, and oil.

13. Before adding the oil to a mayonnaise, first
    a. whip the yolks until lightened.
    b. whisk the yolks with a little lemon juice or vinegar to loosen them.
    c. heat the yolks over a bain marie.
    d. add the seasonings and garnish ingredients.

14. A properly prepared mayonnaise should
    a. have a creamy and sauce-like consistency.
    b. be firm and smooth.
    c. have a mild and balanced flavor.
    d. break down into its component parts after a period of resting, like any other temporary emulsion.

15. When selecting and preparing greens for salad, bear in mind that
    a. prepacked and prewashed greens do not need to be rinsed.
    b. hydroponically-raised greens do not need to be rinsed.
    c. all greens should be quickly and carefully rinsed under running water.
    d. all greens should be rinsed thoroughly in plenty of cold water – several times, if necessary.

Fill in the Blank
For each space, insert the most appropriate response

16. The challenge of making a good _____ lies in achieving balance: the point at which the _____ of the vinegar or juice is tempered but not dominated by the _____ of the oil.

17. White vinegar is often used in mayonnaise because it _____, _____, and _____.

18. A key piece of equipment in salad making is the _____, which uses _____ to remove water from greens so that they _____ and so _____.

19. _____ is a cold sauce typically made from _____ parts oil to_____part vinegar.

20. _____ is the outer portion of the fruit's peel or rind and contains the flavorful _____; it does not include the _____, which has a _____ taste.

Matching
Select the single best match for each item

_____ 21. Lecithin   a. Mayonnaise
_____ 22. Salmonella   b. Croutons
_____ 23. Warm dressing   c. Egg yolks
_____ 24. Temporary emulsion d. Vinaigrette
_____ 25. Rusks   e. Composed salad
_____ 26. Careful arrangement f. Salade tiède

Essay/Short Answer
Answer each question as fully as possible

27. Why does mayonnaise break? Can it be fixed? If so, how?

_____
_____
_____
_____
_____

28. How is a green salad dressed?

_____
_____
_____
_____
_____
_____

29. What is citrus zest? Why is it often blanched before using, and how is the blanching done?

_____
_____
_____
_____
_____
_____

30. What is the procedure for cutting melon balls?

_____
_____
_____
_____
_____
_____

31. List the four principles for constructing a composed salad.

_____
_____
_____
_____
_____
_____

CHAPTER 28

SANDWICHES

Chapter Overview

Sandwiches find a home on nearly every menu, from elegant receptions and teas to substantial but casual meals. Built from four simple elements – bread, a spread, a filling, and a garnish – they exemplify the ways in which a global approach to cuisine can result in nearly endless variety.

Chapter Objectives

After reading and studying this chapter, you will be able to:

➤ Name the basic components of a sandwich and describe the function of each component in the finished sandwich

➤ Describe some of the ways that sandwiches can be presented

➤ Select sandwich shapes to maximize yield and lower food cost

➤ Organize your work station to prepare and serve sandwiches for maximum productivity and efficiency

Study Outline

Elements in a Sandwich

Key Terms and Concepts

bread	buns	closed
club	cold	deli-style
fat-based spread	filling	garnish
grilled	hot	open-faced
Pullman loaf	rolls	spread
toasting	wrappers	

Presentation Styles

Key Terms and Concepts

closed	club	open-faced
uniformity	yield	

Sandwich Production Guidelines

Key Terms and Concepts

assemble	direct line	organize
portioning	slicing	spreadable consistency
toasting		

Chapter 28 Exercises

True/False

Indicate whether each of the following statements is True (T) or False (F)

_____ 1. Spreads add moisture and flavor to a sandwich.

_____ 2. Garnishes help to hold the sandwich together as it is picked up and eaten.

_____ 3. When the spread is combined with the filling in sandwich preparation, there is no need for a spread to be applied to the bread.

_____ 4. To maximize the work flow and eliminate unnecessary movement, organize the work in a circular motion so that it moves counter-clockwise.

_____ 5. If bread must be toasted in advance, it should be held in a warm area, loosely covered.

_____ 6. A fat-based spread provides a barrier to keep the bread from getting soggy.

_____ 7. A finger sandwich served as an hors d'oeuvre is a type of club sandwich.

_____ 8. Grilled sandwiches can be assembled in advance of service and then grilled or heated to order.

_____ 9. A grilled cheese sandwich would be an example of a hot, closed sandwich.

Multiple Choice

Circle the single best answer for each

10. In sandwich making, pâté is used as a
    a. bread.
    b. spread.
    c. filling.
    d. garnish.

11. In sandwich making, guacamole is used as a

    a. bread.
    b. spread.
    c. filling.
    d. garnish.

12. In sandwich making, sprouts are used as a

    a. bread.
    b. spread.
    c. filling.
    d. garnish.

13. When organizing sandwich mise en place, spreads should be

    a. at room temperature.
    b. prepared in advance.
    c. prepared à la minute.
    d. spread on the bread in advance.

14. When organizing sandwich mise en place for maximum efficiency, fillings should be

    a. always well chilled.
    b. portioned in advance.
    c. always cooked in advance.
    d. combined with the spread.

Fill in the Blank

For each space, insert the most appropriate response

15. Tea and finger sandwiches must be made on _____ in order to be _____ and _____ that can be eaten in about _____.

16. Spreads can be _____ and _____, or they may themselves bring a _____ to the sandwich.

17. A _____ provides a barrier to keep the _____ from getting _____.

18. Whenever possible, _____, _____, or _____ breads when ready to assemble the sandwich.

19. Garnishes may be placed either _____ or _____.

Matching

Select the single best match for each item

_____	20. Grilled vegetables	a. Bread
_____	21. Sliced pickle	b. Spread
_____	22. Three slices of bread	c. Filling
_____	23. Rice paper wrapper	d. Garnish
_____	24. Precisely cut	e. Club sandwich
_____	25. Pesto	f. Tea sandwich

Essay/Short Answer

Answer each question as fully as possible

26. What is the most appropriate type of bread for tea and finger sandwiches and why?

_____
_____
_____
_____
_____
_____

27. Describe the functions of a spread in a sandwich.

_____
_____
_____
_____
_____
_____

28. What steps are included in the proper organization of the work station for volume sandwich production?

_____
_____
_____
_____
_____
_____

29. Why is the proper cutting of sandwich shapes so important? Why are "shaped" sandwiches often more expensive to make?

_____

_____

_____

_____

_____

_____

30. "Sandwich fillings are the focus of the sandwich." Explain this statement.

_____

_____

_____

_____

_____

_____

CHAPTER 29

HORS D'OEUVRE AND APPETIZERS

Chapter Overview

The distinction between an hors d'oeuvre and an appetizer has more to do with the portion size and how and when it is served than with the actual food being served. Hors d'oeuvre are typically served as a prelude to a meal, while appetizers are usually the meal's first course.

Chapter Objectives

After reading and studying this chapter, you will be able to:

➤ Describe the roles played by both hors d'oeuvre and appetizers in a meal

➤ Select and prepare ingredients, preparations, and garnishes for hors-d'oeuvre, appetizers, and cold savory mousses

➤ Describe the qualities of foods to be served as appetizers

➤ Present hors-d'oeuvre properly

➤ Name the basic guidelines for preparing and preserving appetizers

➤ Work properly with gelatin in order to achieve specific effects

Study Outline

Hors-d'Oeuvre

Key Terms and Concepts

buffet	butler-style service	chafing dish
hors d'oeuvre	size	

Appetizers

Key Terms and Concepts

appetizer	"building a menu"	composition
garnish	hors d'oeuvre	hot appetizers
portion	salad	seasoning
shared appetizers	vegetables	warm appetizers

Cold Savory Mousse

Key Terms and Concepts

aerator
binder
delicate gel
gel strength
mousse
sliceable gel

aspic
bloom
firm gel
gelatin
mousseline

base
coating gel
forcemeat
lightener
rain

Chapter 29 Exercises

True/False

Indicate whether each of the following statements is True (T) or False (F)

_____ 1. With very few exceptions, hors-d'oeuvre should not require a knife.

_____ 2. With very few exceptions, appetizers should not require a knife.

_____ 3. If the aerator is overwhipped, the mousse may start to deflate from its own weight.

_____ 4. If a purée of vegetables is used in mousse preparation, it may need to be sautéed to reduce the moisture content.

_____ 5. The correct ratio of gel to liquid for preparing cold mousse is .25 ounce gel to 1 pint liquid.

_____ 6. The correct gel strength for preparing cold mousse is firm gel.

_____ 7. The base for a cold savory mousse should be chilled before the melted gelatin is added to it.

_____ 8. Gelatin granules will dissolve in liquid warmed to 110 to 120°F/43 to 49°C.

_____ 9. If a menu features a lobster bisque, it would probably be inappropriate to precede the meal with lobster canapés.

_____ 10. Beaten egg whites and whipped cream are examples of aerators or lighteners.

Multiple Choice

Circle the single best answer for each

11. Gelatin is added to mousse when the
    a. mousse must be held overnight.
    b. base contains a great deal of moisture.
    c. base is not dense enough to give the finished product sufficient structure.
    d. mousse will be served from a buffet.

12. In a mousse preparation, puréed cooked meat would be an example of
    a. base.
    b. binder.
    c. lightener.
    d. stabilizer.

13. In a mousse preparation, beaten egg whites would be an example of
    a. base.
    b. binder.
    c. lightener.
    d. stabilizer.

14. In a mousse preparation, gelatin would serve as the
    a. base.
    b. binder.
    c. lightener.
    d. aerator.

15. Which of the following would *not* be suitable as an hors d'oeuvre?
    a. Caviar
    b. Smoked fish
    c. Grilled vegetable canapés
    d. Caesar salad

Fill in the Blank

For each space, insert the most appropriate response

16. Foods served as hors d'oeuvre should be _____, _____, and _____.

17. To ensure that hot hors d'oeuvre stay hot, avoid _____ and have _____ available for buffet service.

18. Most appetizers are _____, meant to _____ to permit _____.

19. _____, _____, and _____ play a role in the overall composition of the appetizer plate.

20. The concentration of gelatin, or _____ , in a given liquid is usually described in terms of ounces per gallon; _____ is the weakest and _____ is the strongest.

Matching
Select the single best match for each item

_____ 21. Delicate gel   a. Edible chaud-froid

_____ 22. Coating gel   b. Cream cheese

_____ 23. Sliceable gel   c. Cold mousse

_____ 24. Firm gel   d. Egg whites

_____ 25. Base   e. Head cheese

_____ 26. Aerator   f. Jellied consommé

Essay/Short Answer
Answer each question as fully as possible

27. List five guidelines for presenting hors d'oeuvre.

_____

_____

_____

_____

_____

_____

28. How is gelatin used? What is gel strength?

_____

_____

_____

_____

_____

29. How is sheet gelatin bloomed?

_____

_____

_____

_____

30. Describe two methods of melting bloomed gelatin and adding it to the base.

_____

_____

_____

_____

_____

_____

31. Describe the characteristics of a properly made cold savory mousse.

_____

_____

_____

_____

_____

_____

CHAPTER **30**

CHARCUTERIE AND GARDE MANGER

Chapter Overview

Charcuterie, strictly speaking, refers to certain foods made from the pig, including sausage, smoked ham, bacon, head cheese, pâtés, and terrines. Garde manger, traditionally referred to as the kitchen's pantry or larder section, is where foods are kept cold during extended storage and while being prepared as a cold plate.

Chapter Objectives

After reading and studying this chapter, you will be able to:

➢ Define charcuterie and garde manger

➢ Explain what a forcemeat is

➢ Select and prepare ingredients, preparations, and equipment necessary to prepare a variety of forcemeats and forcemeat-based dishes

➢ Sample a forcemeat by preparing a quenelle

➢ Name and describe four forcemeats

➢ Fill and line a mold for terrines and pâtés

➢ Evaluate the quality of finished items prepared from forcemeats

Study Outline

Forcemeats

Key Terms and Concepts

aspic	aspic gelée	binder
country-style forcemeat	die	dominant meat
drum sieve	emulsion	fat
fatback	feed tube	fiber
forcemeat	galantine	gratin forcemeat
grinder	ice bath	liner
molds	mousseline-style forcemeat	panada
pâté	pâté en croûte	quenelle
salt	sanitation	seasoning
sinew	straight forcemeat	tamper
terrine	worm	

Chapter 30 Exercises

True/False

Indicate whether each of the following statements is True (T) or False (F)

_____ 1. Some forcemeats are processed in a food processor to remove any fibers or sinew.

_____ 2. To prepare the meat for grinding, cut it into strips or cubes.

_____ 3. If a prepared forcemeat has a rubbery or tough consistency when tested, heavy cream should be added.

_____ 4. Quenelles are shaped using two spoons.

_____ 5. When using a grinder, the tamper is used to force the meat through the feed tube.

_____ 6. Besides being used to taste test forcemeat, quenelles can be used for other appetizer preparations and in soup.

_____ 7. If a prepared forcemeat does not hold together properly when tested, it may be necessary to add a crust or liner to the mold.

_____ 8. A flour panada can be made by enriching 1 pint of a very heavy béchamel with three to four egg yolks.

_____ 9. Nonfat dry milk powder may be used to replace some or all of the heavy cream in forcemeat recipes.

_____ 10. When grinding all but very delicate meats, begin with a die that has large or medium openings and continue to grind through progressively smaller die until the correct consistency is achieved.

Multiple Choice

Circle the single best answer for each

11. The very fine texture of mousseline forcemeat is achieved by
    a. progressive grindings beginning with a die that has a large opening.
    b. the addition of salt to the forcemeat.
    c. heavy cream and eggs.
    d. sieving.

12. Quenelles are
   a. a type of forcemeat panada.
   b. a type of lined forcemeat.
   c. forcemeat baked in a special mold.
   d. forcemeat dumplings.

13. Panada is a type of
   a. gelatin mix.
   b. liner.
   c. binder.
   d. forcemeat.

14. Pâte à choux is sometimes used in forcemeat preparation to
   a. line the mold.
   b. bind the forcemeat.
   c. form the quenelles.
   d. coat the baked forcemeat terrine.

15. Pâté dough for baking pâté en croûte is:
   a. more delicate than pie dough.
   b. the same as pie dough.
   c. made from pâte à choux.
   d. stronger than pie dough.

Fill in the Blank

For each space, insert the most appropriate response

16. The three basic components of a forcemeat are _____, _____, and _____, especially _____.

17. The five types of forcemeat are _____, _____, _____, _____ and _____.

18. When preparing forcemeat, all ingredients should be chilled to _____ both to prevent _____ and to encourage the _____.

19. To keep the forcemeat properly chilled while mixing the ingredients, use _____ and _____.

20. A _____ is made by soaking cubed bread in milk. A _____ is essentially a heavy béchamel enriched with egg yolks.

Matching

Select the single best match for each item

_____ 21. Dominant meat   a. Provides richness and smoothness

_____ 22. Fat   b. Strengthened clarified stock

_____ 23. Salt   c. Provides flavor and body

_____ 24. Binder   d. Flour or bread

_____ 25. Panada   e. Nonfat dry milk powder

_____ 26. Aspic gelée   f. Helps develop the texture and bind

Essay/Short Answer

Answer each question as fully as possible

27. What is forcemeat? What are the three basic components of a forcemeat? Describe the role of each.

28. What are the five types of forcemeat? Describe each.

29. Why might additional binders be used in a forcemeat? List some typical binders. How are bread and flour panadas made?

30. Describe the process by which forcemeats are evaluated for flavor and consistency.

_____

_____

_____

_____

_____

31. How is a pâté en croûte mold lined?

_____

_____

_____

_____

_____

CHAPTER 31

Chapter Overview

To be successful in the baking and pastry arts, it is important to have a basic understanding of how baking ingredients function and how they react to one another. Knowledge of these principles and processes will not only help you follow any formula and produce better-quality products, but it will also help you develop your own formulas.

Chapter Objectives

After reading and studying this chapter, you will be able to:

➤ Describe the different functions of ingredients in baked items, such as stability, tenderness, and leavening

➤ Explain the importance of accurate measurements in baking

➤ Scale dry and wet ingredients properly, using appropriate measuring equipment

➤ Sift dry ingredients properly

➤ Select and prepare pans and ovens for a variety of baked goods

➤ Cook sugar to various stages to make simple syrup or caramel

➤ Whip cream and egg whites to a range of peaks

➤ Name the basic types of meringues and prepare meringues according to the proper method

Study Outline

Stabilizers

Key Terms and Concepts

arrowroot	bloom	cornstarch
egg	framework	gel
gelatin	gelatinization	gluten
gluten-to-starch ratio	leavening	partial coagulation
pectin	protein coagulation	stabilizer
starch	tapioca	thickener
toughener		

Liquefiers

Key Terms and Concepts

crumb
lactic acid
liquefier
shortening agent
thinner

elasticity
lactose
loosen
sugar
water

fat
leavening
milk
tenderizer

Leaveners

Key Terms and Concepts

acid
baking powder
chemical leavener
double-acting baking powder
mechanical leavener
sourdough starter

active dry yeast
baking soda
compressed yeast
fresh yeast
organic leavener
steam

alkali
biological leavener
crumb
instant yeast
quick bread
yeast

Scaling

Key Terms and Concepts

measure

scale

weigh

Sifting Dry Ingredients

Key Terms and Concepts

aerate
sift

blend

impurities

Cooking Sugar

Key Terms and Concepts

acid
dry method
hard crack
simple syrup
sugar
wet method

caramel
firm ball
recrystallization
soft ball
syrup

crystallization
hard ball
seed
soft crack
thread

Whipping Cream

Key Terms and Concepts

chantilly cream
soft peak

heavy cream
stiff peak

medium peak
whip

Whipping Egg Whites and Making Meringues

Key Terms and Concepts

common meringue	egg whites	egg yolks
foam	Italian meringue	leavener
medium peak	meringue	overbeaten
separation	soft peak	stabilize
stiff peak	Swiss meringue	

Choosing and Preparing Pans

Key Terms and Concepts

batter	film	flour
grease	parchment paper	

Chapter 31 Exercises

True/False

Indicate whether each of the following statements is True (T) or False (F)

_____ 1. A Swiss meringue is prepared by beating the egg whites to soft peaks and then gradually adding a hot sugar syrup.

_____ 2. Steam is the leavening agent in sponge cakes and soufflés.

_____ 3. Angel food cake is baked in an ungreased pan to allow the batter to adhere to the pan.

_____ 4. Sugar syrup stages are tested by dropping a small amount of cooked sugar in lukewarm water and observing how it reacts.

_____ 5. Ingredients should be sifted before they are scaled.

_____ 6. Common meringues are not egg-safe and must be cooked before serving.

_____ 7. The nutty, roasted flavor characteristic of good caramel is best achieved through the wet method.

_____ 8. The protein in flour enables it to act as a stabilizer.

_____ 9. The protein in eggs enable them to act as stabilizers.

_____ 10. The yeast in an unopened package of active dry or instant yeast is in a completely dormant stage and may be stored in an unopened package indefinitely.

Multiple Choice

Circle the single best answer for each

11. A meringue that is prepared by beating the egg whites to soft peaks and then gradually adding a hot sugar syrup is called a/an
    a. common meringue.
    b. Italian meringue.
    c. English meringue.
    d. Swiss meringue.

12. The type of thickener used to produce light, delicate foams that are firmly set, such as Bavarian creams, is
    a. arrowroot.
    b. flour.
    c. pectin.
    d. gelatin.

13. Which common thickener is derived from fruit?
    a. Arrowroot.
    b. Flour.
    c. Pectin.
    d. Gelatin.

14. Baking soda and baking powder are examples of which type of leavener?
    a. Chemical.
    b. Organic.
    c. Physical.
    d. Mechanical.

15. Sourdough starter is an example of which type of leavener?
    a. Chemical.
    b. Organic.
    c. Physical.
    d. Mechanical.

Fill in the Blank

For each space, insert the most appropriate response

16. The most common chemical leaveners are _____ and _____.

17. _____ refers to the characteristic texture of baked goods, caused by the expansion of _____ within the product.

18. Dry ingredients are sifted primarily for three reasons: _____, _____ and _____.

19. When caramelizing sugar, stop the cooking process by _____ just before it reaches the _____.

20. Chantilly cream is made by adding _____ and _____ to whipped cream.

Matching
Select the single best match for each item

_____ 21. Flour   a. Mechanical leavener

_____ 22. Milk   b. Stabilizer

_____ 23. Fat   c. Biological leavener

_____ 24. Steam   d. Chemical leavener

_____ 25. Sourdough starter   e. Liquefier

_____ 26. Double-acting baking powder   f. Shortening agent

Essay/Short Answer
Answer each question as fully as possible

27. Describe how sugar is cooked using the dry method.

_____
_____
_____
_____
_____
_____

28. What is the process for making a Swiss meringue? How is it used?

_____
_____
_____
_____
_____

29. Explain why and when ingredients should be sifted.

_____
_____
_____
_____
_____

30. What are the functions of water and milk in baking?

_____

_____

_____

_____

_____

_____

31. Describe the medium-peak stage in whipping cream.

_____

_____

_____

_____

_____

_____

CHAPTER **32**

YEAST BREADS

Chapter Overview
Breads and rolls made from yeast-raised doughs and batters have a distinct aroma and flavor, produced by the biological process of the yeast's fermentation. The effects vary from the simplicity of a hearth-baked pizza to a delicate egg-and-butter-enriched brioche.

Chapter Objectives
After reading and studying this chapter, you will be able to:
➢ Name two basic categories of yeast doughs

➢ Select and prepare ingredients used to prepare yeast doughs

➢ Prepare a yeast dough

➢ Scale and shape prepared dough to produce loaves, rolls, and other shapes

Study Outline
Lean and Enriched Dough

Key Terms and Concepts

baguette	baking	banneton
biological leavener	boule	bulk fermentation
clean-up period	cooling	couche
development period	eggs	enriched dough
fat	fermentation	final fermentation
final gluten development	flour	folding over
lean dough	pick-up period	preshaping
proof box	proofing	resting
scaling	scoring	shaping
sugar	wash	yeast

Chapter 32 Exercises
True/False
Indicate whether each of the following statements is True (T) or False (F)

_____ 1.   Loaves of bread baked with yeast should be wrapped while still warm to preserve moisture.

_____ 2.   Lean doughs should be baked in a hot oven with steam.

_____ 3. Scoring patterns for oblong loaves are on the loaves' highest points.

_____ 4. In bread production, salt is a flavoring ingredient that may be omitted without any significant impact on the dough.

_____ 5. To proof yeast, combine the yeast with warm liquid and a small amount of flour or sugar.

_____ 6. Wheat flour is the basis for most yeast-raised doughs because it has a low percentage of protein.

_____ 7. Doughs should be left uncovered during bulk fermentation and covered during proofing.

_____ 8. Egg wash should be applied after preshaping but before resting.

_____ 9. Relatively speaking, yeast doughs may be divided into two categories: unleavened doughs and leavened doughs.

_____ 10. The way a pan is prepared depends on the type of dough to be baked.

Multiple Choice

Circle the single best answer for each

11. In order for active dry yeast to grow properly, water, milk, or other liquids used in bread formula should fall within a temperature range of
    a. 40° to 45°F/4° to 6°C.
    b. 68° to 76°F/20° to 24°C.
    c. 105° to 110°F/40° to 43°C.
    d. 120° to 125°F/49° to 52°C.

12. When preparing a pan for lean dough, one appropriate method is to
    a. grease the pan.
    b. grease and line the pan with parchment.
    c. dust the pan with cornmeal.
    d. make no preparations: simply place the prepared dough into the pan.

13. After the first fermentation period, dough should be carefully folded to
    a. release the carbon dioxide.
    b. allow the strands of gluten to relax.
    c. incorporate any flavoring ingredients.
    d. allow it to be mixed properly.

14. Once the dough is scaled, it should rest briefly before being shaped in order to
    a. allow the release of carbon dioxide.
    b. allow the strands of gluten to relax.
    c. allow time to prepare the pans.
    d. brush with egg wash or milk, if using.

15. After bulk fermentation, the dough
    a. is ready to be mixed.
    b. should be baked immediately.
    c. should rest briefly before scaling.
    d. will have doubled in size.

Fill in the Blank
For each space, insert the most appropriate response

16. Lean doughs can be produced with only _____, _____, _____, and _____.

17. The viability of yeast may be tested by _____; if no _____ develops, the yeast should be discarded.

18. Proof and proofing are terms used to describe both _____ and the _____.

19. Scale and scaling are terms used to describe both _____ and _____.

20. In order for compressed or fresh yeast to grow properly, water, milk, or other liquids used in the bread formula should fall within a temperature range of _____.

Matching
Select the single best match for each item

_____ 21. Baguette   a. Bulk fermentation
_____ 22. Brioche   b. Example of lean dough
_____ 23. Pick-up period   c. Example of enriched dough
_____ 24. Final gluten development   d. Dough is smooth and elastic
_____ 25. Development period   e. Dough pulls away from sides of bowl
_____ 26. First fermentation period   f. Dough forms a rough mass

Essay/Short Answer
Answer each question as fully as possible

27. What are the two basic categories of yeast doughs? List the typical ingredients in each.

_____

_____

_____

_____

_____

28. What is scoring? Explain how and why it is used.

_____

_____

_____

_____

_____

29. After the loaves are baked, how should they be handled and why

_____

_____

_____

_____

_____

30. List the seven basic stages of yeast dough, in order.

_____

_____

_____

_____

_____

31. Why and when is dough folded over? How should it be done?

_____

_____

_____

_____

_____

CHAPTER 33

PASTRY DOUGHS AND BATTERS

Chapter Overview

Most pastry doughs and batters contain many common ingredients: flour, fat, liquid, and eggs. What makes each unique is the proportion in which each of the ingredients are used in relation to each other, the flavorings used, and the method for mixing or combining the ingredients.

Chapter Objectives

After reading and studying this chapter, you will be able to:

➤ Name and describe the basic mixing methods for a variety of baked goods

➤ Select and prepare ingredients and equipment for each of the following methods: rubbed-dough, blending, laminating, creaming, and foaming

➤ Create a variety of baked goods using the basic methods discussed in the text

Study Outline

Rubbed-Dough Method

Key Terms and Concepts

cutting-in	flaky	mealy
overwork	rubbed-dough	solid fat
well		

Blending Method

Key Terms and Concepts

batter	blending	chemical leavener
just combined	liquid fat	overmix

Laminated Doughs

Key Terms and Concepts

envelope	folding	gluten
initial dough	lamination	lamination fat
lock-in	phyllo dough	roll-in
single fold	three fold	

The Creaming Method

Key Terms and Concepts

chemical leavener	creaming	incorporation
pliable fat	scraping	

The Foaming Method

Key Terms and Concepts

angel food cake	chiffon cake	cold foaming
foaming	folding	separated foaming
simple syrup	spongy	warm foaming

Pâte à Choux

Key Terms and Concepts

pastry bag	pâte à choux	piping

Guidelines for Shaping and Baking Cookies

Key Terms and Concepts

cookies	drop cookies	molded cookies
piped cookies	rolled and cut cookies	scoop
stenciled cookies	tuiles	twice-baked cookies

Chapter 33 Exercises

True/False

Indicate whether each of the following statements is True (T) or False (F)

_____ 1. Rubbing fat in a mixture until the pieces are the size of shelled walnuts will result in a mealy pie dough.

_____ 2. In the rubbed-dough method, butter is kept cold to inhibit it from easily blending with the flour.

_____ 3. In the rubbed-dough method, if a chemical leavener is used, it should be incorporated while laminating the dough.

_____ 4. The key to a successful blending method is to avoid overmixing the batter.

_____ 5. Convection ovens are particularly good for baking many kinds of cookies.

_____ 6. For the warm foaming method, the eggs and sugar are heated to 120°F/49°C to dissolve the sugar.

_____ 7. Baked items made using the foaming method should be spongy with no discernible crumb and a moist texture.

_____ 8. Baked items made using the rubbed-dough method should have a moist, cake-like texture.

_____ 9. Both angel food cakes and chiffon cakes are made by variants of the foaming method.

_____ 10. When using the blending method, only liquid fats may be used.

Multiple Choice

Circle the single best answer for each

11. Angel food cake is an example of an item prepared by the
    a. blending method.
    b. rubbed-dough method.
    c. foaming method.
    d. creaming method.

12. Biscuits are an example of an item prepared by the
    a. straight-mix method.
    b. rubbed-dough method.
    c. foaming method.
    d. creaming method.

13. The most commonly used leavener for items prepared by the blending or creaming method is
    a. chemical.
    b. mechanical.
    c. organic.
    d. biological.

14. When mixing ingredients using the rubbed-dough method, the fat should be
    a. melted, then cooled.
    b. creamed with the sugar.
    c. room temperature.
    d. chilled.

15. Laminating dough serves to
    a. provide extra sheen to the finished product.
    b. protect the dough from high oven temperatures.
    c. add extra layers and flakiness to the finished product.
    d. strengthen the dough and make it less brittle.

Fill in the Blank

For each space, insert the most appropriate response

16. Pie crust is an example of a preparation using the _____ method; the specific subgroup of this method is _____.

17. The act of beating _____ into the _____ produces the desired texture in baked goods made with the creaming method.

18. The lock-in for a laminated dough has two steps: the _____ and the _____.

19. Most drop cookie doughs are prepared by the _____ or _____ methods.

20. When properly prepared and baked, pâte à choux has a _____ because of the high proportion of _____.

Matching

Select the single best match for each item

_____ 21. Profiterole   a. Rubbed dough
_____ 22. Roll-in   b. Pâte à choux
_____ 23. Tuile   c. Molded and sliced cookie
_____ 24. Biscotti   d. Laminated dough
_____ 25. Scone   e. Stenciled cookie
_____ 26. Danish   f. Lamination fat

Essay/Short Answer

Answer each question as fully as possible

27. What are the three basic types of foaming method? Describe each and list two baked goods which use variants of the foaming method, as discussed in the text.

_____

_____

_____

_____

_____

28. Explain the terms "mealy" and "flaky" as they apply to the rubbed-dough method.

_____

_____

_____

29. How should the wet and dry ingredients be combined, using the blending method?

_____

_____

_____

_____

_____

_____

30. What is the most important factor in making a laminated dough and why? How does this affect the rolling process?

_____

_____

_____

_____

_____

_____

31. What is pâte à choux? List its ingredients and describe the properly-baked final product.

_____

_____

_____

_____

_____

_____

CHAPTER 34

CUSTARDS, CREAMS, AND MOUSSES

Chapter Overview
When baked, eggs, milk, and sugar result in a smooth and creamy baked custard. When stirred together over gentle heat, these same ingredients become vanilla sauce. Starches or gelatin can be included to produce textures that range from thick but spoonable to a sliceable cream. Folding meringue or whipped cream into the custard or cream produces a cold mousse, Bavarian, or Diplomat cream. For a soufflé, meringue is folded into a base and baked until it rises high for one of the most dramatic of all desserts.

Chapter Objectives
After reading and studying this chapter, you will be able to:
➢ Make a baked custard and identify two methods of making its base

➢ Describe and make a stirred custard and custard ice cream

➢ Describe and make a number of mousses

Study Outline
Baked Custard

Key Terms and Concepts

bain-marie	baked custard	cold method
hot water bath	molds	warm method

Stirred Custards, Creams, and Puddings

Key Terms and Concepts

coagulation	coat	cream
curdle	custard	custard ice cream
nappé	pudding	starch
temper		

Mousse

Key Terms and Concepts

aerate

egg-safe

mousse

cream

flavoring ingredients

stabilizer

deflate

meringue

Chapter 34 Exercises

True/False

Indicate whether each of the following statements is True (T) or False (F)

_____ 1. Crème caramel should be allowed to rest overnight or up to 24 hours after baking to allow the caramel to liquefy into a sauce.

_____ 2. Starch-thickened creams and custards must be brought to the full boil.

_____ 3. Baked custards should be allowed to cool in the bain-marie in which they were baked.

_____ 4. A properly prepared mousse should be at the stage of nappé.

_____ 5. The cold method of mixing a custard base is most appropriate for small batches.

_____ 6. When making a stirred custard, temper the hot milk into the egg mixture to produce a smooth sauce.

_____ 7. Allow the base of a custard ice cream to mature in the refrigerator for several hours before freezing for a better consistency.

_____ 8. When making vanilla sauce, the milk should never be brought to the boil; if it gets too hot, the eggs will coagulate.

_____ 9. To check a baked custard for doneness, gently insert a skewer into its center.

Multiple Choice

Circle the single best answer for each

10. To prevent a skin from forming on the surface of a finished stirred custard,
    a. immediately refrigerate it.
    b. place a piece of plastic wrap on the surface.
    c. stir it as it cools in an ice-water bath.
    d. stir it as it cooks at room temperature.

11. The temperature of a cooking vanilla sauce should not exceed
    a. 145°F/63°C.
    b. 180°F/82°C.
    c. 40°F/4°C.
    d. 100°F/38°C.

12. The stage at which vanilla sauce coats the back of the spoon is known as
    a. sabayon.
    b. pâte à bombe.
    c. nappé.
    d. curdling.

13. To avoid deflating a mousse, use a _____ to add the whites to the yolk mixture.
    a. lifting and folding motion.
    b. whisk.
    c. stirring motion.
    d. stand mixer.

14. A good mousse is
    a. light and foamy.
    b. thick and glossy.
    c. thick and smooth.
    d. light and nappé.

Fill in the Blank
For each space, insert the most appropriate response

15. To make a mousse, an _____ is folded into a _____.

16. In a custard ice cream, sugar performs two functions: _____ and
    _____.

17. When baking a custard, the _____ keeps the heat constant and gentle, resulting in a
    _____ for the final product.

18. For the best results in making a custard ice cream, use a mixture of _____ and _____ to
    avoid having too much _____ in the mix.

19. When the vanilla sauce coats the back of a spoon, it should immediately be _____ and
    _____.

Matching

Select the single best match for each item

_____ 20. Gelatin
_____ 21. Whipped cream
_____ 22. Sabayon
_____ 23. Crème caramel
_____ 24. Vanilla sauce
_____ 25. Bain-marie

a. Stirred
b. Aerator
c. Stabilizer
d. Hot water bath
e. Base
f. Baked

Essay/Short Answer

Answer each question as fully as possible

26. What are the reasons for using a hot water bath for a baked custard?

_____
_____
_____
_____
_____
_____

27. When using starch to thicken a cream or pudding to be cooked on the stovetop, what precaution must be observed and why?

_____
_____
_____
_____
_____
_____

28. What is the basic method for making a vanilla sauce?

_____
_____
_____
_____
_____
_____

29. Describe a well-made mousse.

_____

_____

_____

_____

_____

_____

30. After custards are properly baked and removed from the oven, what is the next step and why?

_____

_____

_____

_____

_____

_____

CHAPTER **35**

FILLINGS, FROSTINGS, AND DESSERT SAUCES

Chapter Overview

There are many options for assembling and finishing a cake or for creating the finishing touches to a plated dessert. In adding these elements, the chef should always be mindful of marrying all the flavors and textures, so that they blend, complement, and enhance each other. In addition to their role as dessert adornments, they are also used as basic components of other items. Fillings, frostings, and sauces can be prepared in a variety of consistencies to complement a range of dessert items: they can be pooled on the plate, or drizzled, spooned, or spread over the main items, cake, or pastry.

Chapter Objectives

After reading and studying this chapter, you will be able to:

➤ Select ingredients for and prepare buttercream

➤ Properly slice, fill, and ice a layer cake

➤ Select and prepare ingredients and equipment for ganache

➤ Identify several applications for ganache

➤ Temper chocolate and discuss the reasons for this procedure

➤ Glaze a variety of dessert items with fondant

➤ Select ingredients for and prepare several types of pies and tarts

➤ Prepare and finish truffles

Study Outline

Buttercream

Key Terms and Concepts

buttercream	cake layers	candy thermometer
filling	icing	Italian buttercream
Italian meringue	metal spatula	seeds
serrated knife	smoothing	soft-ball stage
syrup	turntable	

Ganache

Key Terms and Concepts

chocolate
ganache
heavy ganache
seed method
truffle

chocolate sauce
glaze
light ganache
serrated knife
wire rack

crumb coating
hard ganache
seal coat
tempering chocolate

Working with Fondant

Key Terms and Concepts

éclair
tempering fondant

fondant
wire rack

glaze

Making a Pie or Tart

Key Terms and Concepts

blind baking
cooling racks
custard filling
dusting
lattice crust
overhang
pie
rolling
single-crust pie
toppings

body
cream filling
double-crust pies
egg wash
lining pans
pastry brush
prebaked
scrap dough
starch
vent

chilling
crumb topping
dough
fruit filling
meringue
pastry shell
pudding filling
sheet pans
tart
weights

Making Truffles

Key Terms and Concepts

coat
rolling
truffle

firm
scoop

heavy ganache
tempered chocolate

Chapter 35 Exercises

True/False

Indicate whether each of the following statements is True (T) or False (F)

_____ 1. To temper chocolate with the seed method, chop it into small pieces and melt it over simmering water until it reaches a temperature of 92°F/33°C.

_____ 2. A prepared buttercream should be smooth and soft with no detectable grains of sugar or lumps of butter.

_____ 3. When making an Italian buttercream, if the meringue becomes too hot, it will curdle the eggs as it is added to the rest of the ingredients.

_____ 4. When tempering chocolate, if the temperature drops below 85°F/29°C, the chocolate will become grainy and can no longer be used.

_____ 5. One pound of buttercream will either fill one 10-inch cake or ice one 10-inch cake.

_____ 6. Blind baking is usually done when there is not enough time to prebake the pastry shell before it will be filled.

_____ 7. Crumb toppings should be applied in an even layer over the surface of single-crust pies.

_____ 8. Éclairs are glazed with fondant using a dipping tool to lower the entire item into the warm glaze.

_____ 9. To flavor fondant, paddle the fondant and the desired flavoring agent together in a mixer until mostly combined, then melt the mixture to eliminate any streaks.

Multiple Choice

Circle the single best answer for each

10. A _____ is often applied to cakes that will be glazed.
    a. syrup.
    b. meringue.
    c. temper coat.
    d. seed coat.

11. Buttercreams are typically used as
    a. bases for soufflés.
    b. fillings and icings for cakes.
    c. fillings for Napoleons and eclairs.
    d. glazes for cakes and petit fours.

12. Fondant is typically used as
    a. a base for buttercreams.
    b. fillings and icings for cakes and tortes.
    c. truffles.
    d. a glaze for cakes and petit fours.

13. For fondant to have a glossy and smooth finish, it must be
    a. beaten at room temperature until smooth and shiny.
    b. spread over the item and then the item is chilled to 40°F/4°C.
    c. warmed over simmering water until liquid enough to flow readily.
    d. prepared with superfine or confectioners' sugar.

Fill in the Blank

For each space, insert the most appropriate response

14. When preparing an Italian buttercream, the sugar syrup should reach _____ or be at the _____ stage; when it reaches this temperature, it should be immediately added to the _____.

15. Chocolate truffles are prepared with _____. They may be coated with _____ to give a glossy coating.

16. Cake layers are often brushed with a _____, which adds _____ and _____ to the finished item.

17. As discussed in the text, five uses for ganache are _____, _____, _____, _____, and _____.

18. When baking a double-crusted pie, always _____ in the top crust to _____.

Matching

Select the single best match for each item

_____ 19. Blind baking
_____ 20. Italian meringue
_____ 21. Tempered chocolate
_____ 22. Glazing
_____ 23. Light ganache
_____ 24. Turntable

a. Fondant
b. Truffle
c. Italian buttercream
d. Cake
e. Chocolate sauce
f. Pie or tart shell

Essay/Short Answer

Answer each question as fully as possible

25. Why should chocolate be tempered? What are the characteristics of properly tempered chocolate?

_____

_____

_____

_____

_____

_____

26. Why should fondant be tempered? What are the characteristics of properly tempered fondant?

_____

_____

_____

_____

_____

_____

27. How should dough be prepared and placed into a pie or tart pan?

_____

_____

_____

_____

_____

_____

28. What is the method for making ganache? What are the differences in appearance between warmed ganache to be used as a glaze and whipped ganache to be used as a filling?

_____

_____

_____

_____

_____

_____

29. Describe the process for making an Italian buttercream. What are the characteristics of a properly made buttercream?

_____

_____

_____

_____

_____

CHAPTER 36

PLATED DESSERTS

Chapter Overview
When designing a plated dessert, the chef must consider contrasting and complementing flavors and textures, the color and style, customer base, specific event or menu needs, and the environment for preparation and service. Even with all of this in mind, it is important to realize that a dessert does not have to be complex to be flavorful and memorable. There are a number of simple and easy ways to dress us a basic dessert. Some simple examples are the addition of a warm sauce, a frozen element such as ice cream, or a simple garnish such as tuile, candied nuts, or slices of fruit.

Chapter Objectives
After reading and studying this chapter, you will be able to:
➢ Determine how to identify trends in plated desserts.

➢ Describe contrast in desserts and what roles flavor, taste, texture, temperature, and eye appeal play in a plated dessert.

➢ Select and prepare ingredients, methods, and equipment necessary to prepare a variety of plated desserts.

➢ Identify the techniques, equipment, and set up necessary to create restaurant desserts.

➢ Identify the techniques, equipment, and set up necessary to create banquet desserts.

➢ Describe mise en place and factors to consider when plating frozen desserts.

Study Outline
Plated Desserts

Key Terms and Concepts

aroma	flavor	seasonality trends
banquet dessert	garnish	taste
contrast	plated dessert	temperature
eye appeal	restaurant dessert	texture

Chapter 36 Exercises
True/False
Indicate whether each of the following statements is True (T) or False (F)

_____ 1. Plated desserts must be complex to be truly interesting and flavorful.

_____ 2. Basic desserts, such as a slice of pie, can be dressed up simply by adding a sauce or garnish.

_____ 3. When a restaurant's menu changes, so should the dessert menu.

_____ 4. Serving ice cream with warm chocolate sauce and a tuile is a basic example of contrasting elements in a dessert.

_____ 5. Current trends include advanced, complex, intricately plated desserts.

_____ 6. Most plated desserts can be served in a large-volume setting.

_____ 7. Frozen items should be the first thing plated in a composed dessert.

_____ 8. Dessert menus should change seasonally and with current trends.

Multiple Choice
Circle the single best answer for each

9. Which of the following can help control costs in dessert preperation?
    a. ordering from a wholesale purveyor
    b. featuring seasonal items
    c. never using chocolate
    d. bigger ladles

10. An ideal textural component should have:
    a. a balanced mouthfeel
    b. always a smooth texture
    c. multiple flavoring ingredients
    d. five textures

11. Which of the following is a consideration in contrasting presentation?
    a. shape
    b. color
    c. volume
    d. all of the above

12. Which of the following is not a consideration when altering a plated dessert specifically for a banquet?
    a. equipment needs
    b. storage space
    c. minimalism
    d. timing of service

13. What could be a solution for an item that is not selling well?
    a. change the wording of the dessert on the menu
    b. change the placement of the item on the menu
    c. allow the waitstaff to taste the dessert
    d. all of the above

Fill in the Blank

For each space, insert the most appropriate response

14. The five major components of contrast to consider when preparing a plated dessert are _____, _____, and _____, _____, and _____.

15. Two current trends in plated desserts named in this chapter are _____ and _____.

16. Three simple additions to a dessert to make it a composed plate are_____, _____, and _____.

Matching

Select the single best match for each item

_____ 17. Spice   a. Texture

_____ 18. Cool   b. Temperature

_____ 19. Liquid   c. Flavor and aroma

_____ 20. Volume   d. Presentation

_____ 21. Acidic   e. Seasonality

_____ 22. Spring   f. Taste

Essay/Short Answer

Answer each question as fully as possible

23. Describe the major considerations when determining how to set up a dessert station in a restaurant.

_____

_____

_____

_____

_____

_____

24. Describe the major components of contrast and give an example how each could be utilized in a dessert.

_____

_____

_____

_____

_____

_____